MUSIC THEORY FOR BEGINNERS

ESSENTIAL MUSIC THEORY MADE EASY FOR ALL MUSICIANS

AVENTURAS DE VIAJE

WARNINGS AND DISCLAIMERS

The information in this publication is made public for reference only.

Neither the author, publisher, nor anyone else involved in the production of this publication is responsible for how the reader uses the information or the result of his/her actions.

CONTENTS

THANKS FOR YOUR PURCHASE

Did you know you can get FREE chapters of any SF Nonfiction Book you want?

https://offers.SFNonfictionBooks.com/Free-Chapters

You will also be among the first to know of FREE review copies, discount offers, bonus content, and more.

Go to:

https://offers.SFNonfictionBooks.com/Free-Chapters

Thanks again for your support.

INTRODUCTION

Music theory is the science of music—this science attempts to understand and document the patterns in music, why they exist, and how to bend them to our will. After all, music is a highly advanced and well constructed form of art that involves countless moving parts created from math, physics, and acoustics. Understanding music takes time, patience, and effort—spend 10 minutes researching it and you'll notice that. The beautiful thing about music is that by learning more, it gets easier. It isn't like learning math in school, where one moment you're learning 2x2 and the next you're into calculus. No, music becomes less challenging the further in you get. This guide will help you through those first difficult steps, here we will break through the wall that so many others stop at. Not long from now, you'll look back at this first paragraph with all the tools needed to play, read, and understand music!

What makes this book different from others in music theory, is that instead of catering to experienced musicians, here we are catering to non-musicians. There are no needlessly complicated terms here, no confusing jargon, no assumptions of knowledge. The books in this genre also tend to ignore popular types of music. Many experts like to think that music theory is only for classical and jazz music—I don't. In this book, we'll be covering the topic in a way that allows you to apply it to any genre, any style, and any instrument. It doesn't matter whether you play jazz with a piano, metal with a guitar, or electronic music with a laptop, you'll still be able to apply the things you learn here to your craft.

SO WHAT IS MUSIC THEORY ANYWAY?

If you're here, you are clearly someone that is excited about the concept of music theory. You're excited by this almost mystical concept, but this source of knowledge that has the potential to make you a better musician. A source of knowledge that may even allow you to play like the musicians you look up to. You may be excited by the prospect of spending hours studying concepts, names, music, and working to apply those things. Or you might not be excited for that part, that's fine too. There are very few people who like to struggle, it's human to want the easy way. Now, I'm not saying music theory is easy, but there is definitely an *easier* way to learn it.

What is Music Theory?

From where you stand right now, music theory may seem completely alien to you—distant, intimidating, and very time-consuming. You may feel like you don't want to spend weeks and months of your life learning something that may or may not turn you into the musician you always dreamed of. You may even feel that music theory is something best left to the experts, the professors, and the naturally gifted. It's clearly not meant for us, right? Us lowly musicians who fiddle with our instruments and get excited over things as minor as playing a chord properly. The thought may even cross your mind that learning musical theory is more trouble than it's worth, it may even strike you as something that takes the raw beauty away from music and turns it into a dull science.

Well, you're wrong. This book does not exist to make music theory even more enigmatic, I did not write it to make you struggle more. No, this book exists to make your life easier in every way. Whatever your attitude going into this, you will learn everything you need to become the musician you'd always hoped to be. Instead of sucking up all the fun and creativity out of music, the concepts in this book will allow you to look at music from a perspective you have never seen before. In the same way that a great chef is able to make great food if he knows his craft, a great musician can make great music if he knows his. By learning music theory, you amplify your ability to make incredible music. By knowing what to look for, what flavors compliment each other, and what ingredients to use, you can crank your expressive potential all the way up to 11.

That is musical theory. It is the knowledge of all the tools and ingredients needed to open your horizons as a musician. It's not a textbook that tells you what to do, it rather trains your ear and hands to allow you to better create what you want to create. All theory is harmony, rhythm, and melody—these are the key structures of sound and allow us to organize seemingly random sounds into music. Knowing these key building blocks will make you a better musician.

Why is it Important?

While many people may think that music is something that can start on any note, travel to any place, and end whenever the performer decides, that's not necessarily true. Although it's definitely true that some compositions do follow this path, they are mostly confusing, unpleasant to listen to, and without any form of direction. Musicians that create music like this tend to do it to prove a point or make a statement, rather than actually create music.

To be able to create compositions and improvisations that play and sound great, you need to know your music thoroughly. You need to be able to place notes and chords next to each other in a way that sounds pleasing and makes sense to your audience. And of course, because music is the one universal form of communication, it is pretty important that the music you make, makes sense.

In all honesty, the importance of learning music theory is as much a motivational thing as it is a technical thing. There are times where you feel like you're getting nowhere with your instrument, times where everything just feels a bit overwhelming. Well, those are the perfect times to sit down and read. Focussing solely on technical practising is a path that leads to madness. There is nothing that can equal the feeling you get when you realize that you are able to construct music out of nothing. And, that feeling won't come from only technical practising, you need to have a strong theoretical backing for that.

Keep in mind, as a musician, you only get out as much as you put in. If you want to be able to play along with classical musicians, you need to know how to read by sight and keep a steady tempo. If you want to keep up with your favorite rock stars, you need to know your keys and scales. Understanding music theory is all down to personal discipline and a want to be better. But, in the end, it's all worth it. Playing music is fun, and you'll have infinite fun if you can create your own music.

The History of Music Theory

Greece is known as the cradle of all classical art; regardless of the artform, it probably had some roots in classical Greece. In the year 600 BC, legendary mathematician Pythagoras labeled music a science and defined the octave scale, the cornerstone of much of modern music. Music was an incredibly important part of Greek society, to almost religious levels of reverence. So, when one of their greatest minds decided to start defining it, the musicians of the time soon caught on and added to Pythagoras' findings. By the year 350 BC, Aristotle, another legendary man of science, scientifically analyzed music and created the first mathematical form of notation. A work of sheer genius and forethought that is still studied today.

Music theory subsequently went through a dark age, with the rest of european art, until Boethius came around in the year 521 AD. He revised and revived the ancient Greek system of notation and introduced it to the musicians of western europe as a sophisticated form of musical notation. This allowed musicians, clergymen, and scholars to finally scribe the hymns, laments, and folk songs of their lands.

By the year 600 AD, Pope Gregory commissioned the Schola Cantarum, the world's first school of music. With the backing of the world's most powerful institution of the time, music theory took off to new heights. Within 144 years of the school's foundation, music colleges had sprung up in Paris, Cologne, and Metz.

In 800 AD, Charlemagne, the first Holy Roman Emperor, commissioned the most important poems and psalms of the empire to be set to music and noted down for future generations. This undertaking led to the discovery of modes over the following 50 years, the first major breakthrough in theory since the invention of notation.

Skipping forward 150 years, Guido D'Arezzo made the next great leap forward in music theory by adding time signatures to notation and creating the solfege system. The solfege system being the famous "do re mi fa so la ti do" vocal scale. Without this invention, modern vocalism may be nothing like we know it today.

With the onset of the Renaissance, mankind's greatest era of artistic advancement, the first ever sheets of music were printed. This led to the first pieces of music being organized and produced for profit. And as with everything, money was a powerful force for driving advancement.

The rest is history. Musical theory has consistently grown and evolved since then, but not so much that we can't recognize the genes of modern notation in Boethius' original scribblings.

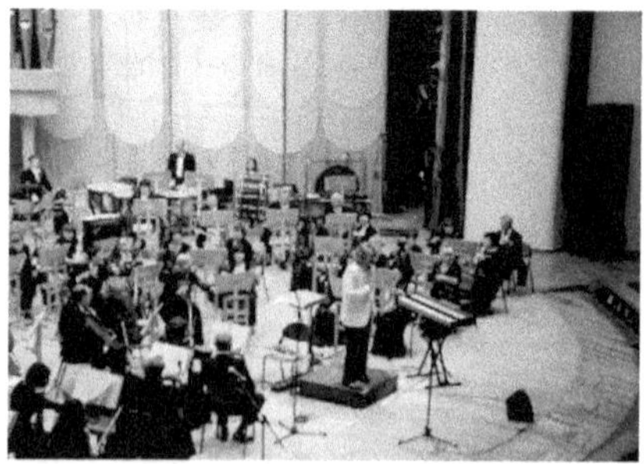

Important Eras in Music

While music has gone through millennia of constant evolution and change, there are some definite eras of massive advancement. Of course, there are more genres of music than one can count, and every region has its own native music, which may make this list seem awfully eurocentric. There is a reason for that eurocentrism though, the musical theory that we use today was developed through these defining eras of European musical advancement. So while musical history is certainly not exclusive to Europe, the history of this brand of musical theory is very much rooted on the European continent.

Baroque

Between the years 1600 and 1760, was the height of the Baroque period of European musical progression. The music of this time was defined by complicated, dramatic, and grandiose orchestral arrangements. This music was the base of all the classical and symphonic music that came after it. This period also produced the most groundbreaking early composers in music theory history, including the likes of Johann Sebastian Bach, George Handel, Antonio Vivaldi, and Claudio Monteverdi.

Classical

Of course, when you hear "classical" used as a term to describe music, you think about large orchestras featuring a conductor and an audience filled with pensioners. While you may think any arrangement that features a large group of musicians playing a complicated instrumental piece is "classical," that term is actually the name for a specific period of musical history rather than a genre. This period existed right after the Baroque period, between 1730 and 1820. The music of this period arose from a tiredness of the pompous and over-the-top sound of baroque music, and favored a more stripped-down, simplistic sound.

The composers of this time put special effort into lowering the amount of instruments in arrangements and dialing down the drama of compositions, in favor of more beautiful and clean sounds. Some of the most famous composers of all time fall into this period and type of music, they include Ludwig Van Beethoven, Wolfgang Amadeus Mozart, Franz Joseph Haydn, and Franz Schubert.

Romantic

As a reaction and rival to the classical period in music, the romantic period came through during the same rough time frame. Between 1815 and 1910, the Romantic era focused on casual, emotional, and expressionist pieces. This form of music revolved around themes of nature, romance, exploration, and spirituality, in a similar way to the storytelling of Opera music. The major composers of this era include Peter Ilich Tchaikovsky, Richard Wagner, Johannes Brahms, and Frederic Chopin.

Modern

Historically, musical compositions always relied heavily on pleasant harmonies, melodies, and simple rhythms. As music entered the 20th century, composers rejected those historically important trends and opted for more abstract and eccentric sounds. Modernist composers, between the years 1890 and 1950, put much more emphasis on unusual meter, dissonance, and minor keys. Some of the most famous composers of this time include Claude Debussy, Igor Stravinsky, Arnold Schoenberg, and Richard Strauss.

Contemporary

Finally having caught up with the current-day, contemporary composers have yet again rejected their immediate past. Many of these composers have left behind many of the unusual fashions of the Modernist era, looking rather towards the earlier Baroque and Classical eras of music. While others have taken the experimentation of the Modernist era into extremes and greater levels of avant-garde. The era that we are in right now, could be considered one of the most experimental and musically liberal that we have seen so far. Whether it be avant-garde, minimalism, postmodernism, or post-minimalism, the different popular styles of the contemporary era varied wildly in sound and composition.

THE FUNDAMENTALS OF MUSIC THEORY

Educating Your Ear

How do you educate your ear? That may sound like a strange thing to suggest, but trust me when I say that an educated ear is a musician's most important tool. Music, in its most simple form, is just a grouping of squiggly waves vibrating through the air. In scientific terms, waves are a disturbance that transfers energy through a medium. There are two common forms of waves that we encounter in our day-to-day life, the first is mechanical and the second is electromagnetic. Mechanical waves need a physical medium to travel through, like a wave through water or a shockwave through air. Electromagnetic waves, on the other hand, are able to travel without a medium, they can transfer their energy through a vacuum like that in space.

Sound

Sound is a mechanical wave, it is a form of pressure that travels and transfers its energy through air which acts as a medium. Scientifically speaking, sound has various unique elements to it, like frequency, duration, volume, and speed. The element which we are most interested in is frequency, which can be explained as the amount of pressure waves transferred over a period of time. Frequency is measured in hertz (Hz), and one hertz means that one wave of pressure has travelled in a second. The higher a frequency is, the more waves travel in that second.

Pitch

In a physical sense, pitch is the frequency of a sound which is produced by a specific object vibrating, like the string on an instrument. The average person has the ability to hear pitches in a relatively wide range of frequencies. This range starts at 20 Hz and stretches up to 20,000 Hz (also written as 20 kHz or kilohertz). Our hearing range will reduce with age and mistreatment though, that's why many professional musicians may suffer hearing problems later in life if not careful. Musically speaking, the pitch of a note is its harmonic value. If a note is higher or lower than another note, that means it's pitch is higher or lower in a harmony. Because of this, studying Harmony is akin to studying pitch.

Notes

A note is the name given to a particular pitch with a specific duration, quality, and volume. The notes in western music theory are named using the first seven letters of the Latin alphabet, from A to G. Each note has an inherent pitch which makes the note what it is. For example, the E4 on a Piano (High E on a Guitar) has a frequency of 329.6 Hz when tuned to standard pitch.

Timbre

It is possible for two sounds to have different rhythms and a different overall sound, but if those two sounds have the same pitch frequency, then they are the same note. What makes those two sounds different to each other, even though they are the same note, is that they have different timbres. The timbre of a sound is the quality of a sound. This doesn't necessarily mean some sounds are 'higher' quality than others, it means that a note produced from a flute and a note produced from a cello may technically be the same note, but because of the instrument and creation of that note, it will sound different.

Tone

Tone has a lot of meanings in music, too many in fact. It is often used interchangeably with many of the terms mentioned above, which can cause a lot of confusion. Tone and timbre often go hand-in-hand. Often when somebody refers to the tone of an instrument, they actually mean the timbre. Tone is also often used to describe a note that is artificially generated to sound steady, pure, and without natural resonance. This type of sound can only be produced digitally or in a completely soundproof room which eliminates all extra vibration and resonance.

Musical Notes

The notes we commonly use in Western music can be compared to the alphabet of a language. These notes can be used to create words, sentences, and entire stories if put together the right way!

In the Western music theory system there are only 12 notes. This 12 note system is by far the most popular around today, and is recognized worldwide as the standard medium for notating music. There are many other systems though, just not nearly as popular. These are usually exclusive to cultural music in regions such as India, China, parts of Africa, and even some extinct cultures such as Byzantium.

The 12 notes we use in Western musical theory are: A, A# (Bb), B, C, C# (Db), D, D# (Eb), E, F, F# (Gb), G, G# (Ab).

I'm sure you've noticed that these notes are named after the first seven letters of the Latin alphabet. Alongside those seven letters, there are also another five notes with a hash symbol (#) next to them. This symbol signifies that the note is sharp, which means it is raised. These sharp notes also have a bracketed counterpart which has a symbol resembling a small "b" next to it, this indicates that the note is lowered.

In the Western system, the sharp of one note is harmonically equivalent to the flat note above it. For example, a C# is the same as a Db, and a D# is the same as an Eb. In two unique cases, E and F as well as B and C, have no flats or sharps between them.

If you were to look at a piano, you would see both black and white keys. The white keys are what are known as natural notes, these are notes which are neither sharp nor flat. The black keys, on the other hand, are always sharp or flat notes. While these keys may sit directly next to each other on a keyboard or a guitar, in theoretical terms they are typically a half step apart from each other.

The distance between A and A# is a half step, the distance between B and C is also a half step because there is no flat or sharp between them. On the other hand, the distance between A and B is a whole step when you skip over a note between them.

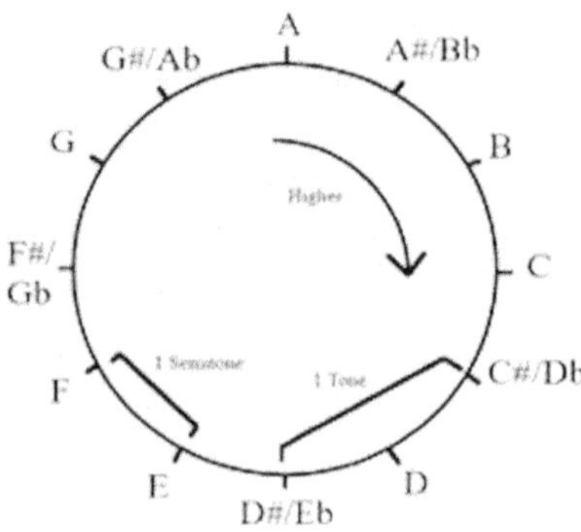

Registry and Octaves

Each note in our system has its own unique pitch. But, as we can see above, there are only 12 notes. Of course, this means that there is a massive range of sound that we can hear which doesn't conform to only those 12 notes. That means that these notes have to cover multiple high and low registers. Every single register includes the same 12 notes, just at a higher or lower pitch.

When a note is played at a lower or higher register, we say that those notes are an octave apart. This means that it has a different pitch but is the same exact note. Simply put, an octave is the distance between a note and its twin higher or lower on the register. If you were to look at the frequency waves of the same note played at two different points on the register, you would note that every octave upwards has double the waves of the octave below it. For every octave down, the amount of frequency waves is halved.

By adding more waves to the note, you increase the pitch. This is why notes higher up the register sound higher, each doubling of waves equals a doubling of pitch.

In the space between octaves you will find all 12 notes in the same order as shown earlier. This means that the pattern for every octave is the same, it's always the same distance between them. Think of it like a clock, if you start at 12pm and go forward 12 hours, you will end up at 12am. Just replace 12pm with A, 1pm with A#, and so on.

Because of limitations in what we can hear, and what our instruments can produce, there are only a certain amount of octaves used in music. Depending on the instrument, the range of octaves can vary massively. Pianos, for instance, can have up to 88 keys covering 7 octaves.

Standard Pitch

When notating the distance between octaves, you will often see a number attached to a note. For example, on a piano there are eight C notes in different registers. The lowest is C1 and the highest is C8. This same logic applies to all notes and helps us to figure out roughly where we need to be playing and how it should sound.

So, the distance between C5 and C6 would then be a full octave, the same goes for A1 to A2, D4 to D5, E6 to E7, etc. The distance between C5 and C7 would also then equal two octaves, and jumping from C5 to C8 would be three octaves. If you were to play an A3, that would be considered in the third range. Similarly, an A4 would be in the fourth range. Each range starts on a C, and the C4 note is known as the middle C because of its position directly in the center of the register.

Octaves, registry, and pitch have been used for centuries to explain how low or high something sounds. But, historically, there was always the issue of not knowing if my A4 was the same as your A4. Before the 19th century, there was no concerted effort to standardize the pitch used across western music. This led to most musicians just picking certain frequencies which sounded right to them, and hoping that it was actually the note they were looking for. Because of this, and other reasons, it became pretty clear that for music theory to continue developing, a standard pitch was necessary.

Over decades of various attempts at standardizing pitch, we eventually settled on the A above middle C at a frequency of 440 Hz. This A4 acts as the reference note, with every other note placed relative to it. Most instruments today are tuned in accordance with this standard tuning. For example, when it comes to standard guitar tuning, A above middle C is located on the 5th fret of the 1st string.

So, we know that A4 is based on a frequency of 440 Hz, but what about one octave higher? A5 is double the frequency of A4 and therefore sits at 880 Hz. Conversely, A3 is half the frequency and sits at 220 Hz.

Dividing Octaves

One full octave can be divided into six whole steps, one step is then divided into two half-steps, and one half-step (semitone) is divided into 100 cents. For example, A and A# are one half-step apart, but that also means that 100 cents separates them. Cents are used to describe miniscule intervals called microtones.

When looking at measurements lower than a semitone, instead of using hertz as the default frequency unit of measure, it is easier and more convenient to use cents. Cents are a logarithmic unit of measure which allows for far easier calculation of pitch difference.

Our ears are very sensitive, in fact we can hear as little as a difference of only a few cents. Although, a one cent difference in pitch is typically too small for the human ear to hear. Depending on the accuracy of your tuning, it is still possible for your instrument to be in tune but sound slightly off. This is the case when your tuning is off pitch by a difference that can only be measured in cents. Correcting that tiny difference in pitch is referred to as fine-tuning and most of the tuners available nowadays, even some mobile apps, do accommodate this type of ultra-accurate tuning. At the end of the day, the more accurately you can tune your instrument to correct pitch, the better it will sound.

Understanding Intervals

What Is an Interval?

An interval is the term given to describe the relationship between two separate notes. It is the distance in harmony between two unique notes and sounds.

Each interval has a different sound and a unique name. Their names stem from their position in diatonic scales, and because of that intervals can either be Major, minor, or perfect. Major and minor intervals are most commonly found in western music, while perfect intervals are typically found in more rudimentary and simple forms of cultural music.

If you take a look at the note circle from earlier, you will see that there is a semitone between each note in the circle. That semitone can be considered a type of interval, in fact, you can begin on any note, and play any other note, and you will always have an interval of some kind between those notes.

There are a number of intervals on our note circle, and in order to walk through them all with you, we need to pick a root note to begin on. This note will be the harmonic center of our chord or scale. For simplicity's sake, we'll use C as the root note here, as it is the root note of the Major scale.

- The first interval on our scale is C to C. The root note actually does have an interval to itself, this is called the Perfect unison.
- Following that, you have C to C#/Db, this is a minor 2nd above C (and a Major 7th below it). This interval is the equivalent of one semitone.
- Then you have C#/Db to D, this is a Major 2nd above C (and a minor 7th below it). This interval is the equivalent of one whole tone.
- Next comes D to D#/Eb, this is a minor 3rd above C (and a Major 6th below it).

- Then we have D#/Eb to E, a Major 3rd above C (and a minor 6th below it).
- Following that, E to F. A Perfect 4th above C (and a Perfect 5th below it), fourth and fifth notes are known as perfect instead of Major or minor because they retain their position and properties regardless of what scale you are playing. Major and minor notes can move around and change, but these notes don't.
- After that, you have F to F#/Gb. This is an Augmented 4th above C (and the same below it), also known as a tritone. This interval is unusual, it is very dissonant and most musicians don't enjoy playing it because it tends to not fit into compositions easily.
- The eighth interval in this scale is F#/Gb to G, a Perfect 5th above C (and a Perfect 4th below it).
- Next comes G to G#/Ab, this is a minor 6th above C (and a Major 3rd below it).
- Then G#/Ab to A, a Major 6th above C (and a minor 3rd below it).
- Followed by A to A#/Bb, a minor 7th above C (and a Major 2nd below it).
- Towards the end of our circle is A#/Bb to B, a Major 7th above C (and a minor 2nd below it).
- And lastly, there is B to C, this is a Perfect octave interval because it is a full octave above the root of C.

With that, we have gone full circle and arrived back on the root note, only one octave higher than where we started.

If you were counting, you'd notice that there were four Major intervals, four minor intervals, 4 Perfect intervals, and one Augmented interval (the tritone). If we were to look at all of the intervals in regards to semitones, we would see this them like this:

- C to C: Perfect unison of zero semitones apart.
- C to C#: minor 2nd of one semitone apart.
- C to D: Major 2nd of two semitones apart.

- C to D#: minor 3rd of three semitones apart.
- C to E: Major 3rd of four semitones apart.
- C to F: Perfect 4th of five semitones apart.
- C to F#: Augmented 4th of six semitones apart.
- C to G: Perfect 5th of seven semitones apart.
- C to G#: minor 6th of eight semitones apart.
- C to A: Major 6th of nine semitones apart.
- C to A#: minor 7th of ten semitones apart.
- C to B: Major 7th of eleven semitones apart.
- C to C: Perfect octave of 12 semitones apart.

Keep in mind, in musical theory, Major and Perfect are always capitalized and minor is not. This goes for the full terms and any abbreviations.

Intervals can be used to express both chords and scales, this is because a specific group of intervals will define a unique sound, a special place in the harmony.

Inverting Intervals

There is another important property to understand in intervals beyond their name and quality. Have a look at the circle of notes above, see how every interval can travel both up and down. Intervals have four possible methods of movement:

- Descending: Higher notes that travel counterclockwise around the circle of notes to a lower pitch, for example E to C#.
- Ascending: Lower notes that travel clockwise around the circle of notes to a higher pitch, for example A to C.
- Unison: When the same note is played twice.
- Harmonic: When multiple notes are played at the same time.

It's possible to say that B is a Major 3rd interval above G, and that Eb is a Major 3rd below G. This means that intervals can be inverted, because B is a Major 3rd above G, then it can also be another interval down from G on the octave below, in this case a minor 6th.

Because of this, intervals come in duos. Every note relationship can be expressed with two intervals, one higher and one lower. You would have noticed the intervals in parenthesis above, those are the inverted intervals for those notes.

To go into more detail, there are always two possible solutions to finding the interval between two notes. For example, let's use A and C. The note C is a certain distance away from A. If C is a higher pitch than A, the interval is ascending. In this situation we would say that C is a minor 3rd above A, this makes C into A's minor 3rd interval.

If the C note in question is lower than the A, then this C is a descending interval. Because of that you can say that C is a Major 6th below A.

When dealing with intervals, unless you have something indicating otherwise, you always assume the lower note to be the root note. This is important to keep in mind because we count intervals clock-wise from the lowest note.

It's surprisingly easy once you get the hang of it. Try figuring out these intervals below:

- F to D (Ascending) = ?
- F to D (Descending) = ?
- A to C# (Ascending, the sharp symbol indicates that this is ascending) = ?
- A to Db (Descending, the flat symbol indicates that this is descending) = ?
- Eb to Gb = ?

Keep in mind, whenever an interval is ascending you will see it expressed with a sharp symbol, and when it is descending it will always have a flat symbol.

Chromatic and Diatonic

Every interval we've covered so far falls under a group known as chromatic intervals. These intervals being *chromatic* means that they relate to the chromatic scale, the set of all 12 notes that we use in the western music system. Chromatic intervals are simply the set of all the intervals that exist between the notes we use today.

Inside of our set of chromatic intervals, you will find a set of intervals known as diatonic intervals. These are the intervals that make up the Major scale, the most important and popular scale in music. Every other scale is compared to or measured against the Major scale in one way or another.

The Major scale is the single most important scale to learn in music. This scale is diatonic, which is why all the intervals inside of it are known as diatonic.

All of the diatonic intervals are as follows:

- Perfect unison C - C
- Major 2nd C - D
- Major 3rd C - E
- Perfect 4th C - F
- Perfect 5th C - G
- Major 6th C - A
- Major 7th C - B

Augmented and Diminished

Aside from Major, minor, and Perfect intervals, we also have Augmented and Diminished intervals. These intervals are seldom seen and are usually only used in music that specifically calls for them.

All scales and chords are made up from separate notes and intervals. We use intervals to help write out and name notes and scales, but there are times, depending on the scale, where we have to change our methods to fit certain rules in music theory. That is when we will use augmented and diminished notes and intervals.

We'll get to these rules as we make our way through this book, but for now just know that diminished intervals lower minor and Perfect intervals by one semitone. Augmented notes, on the other hand, heighten Major and Perfect intervals by one semitone.

The Keystones of Music

Music consists of three keystone properties, harmony, melody, and rhythm. Without these properties, music as we know it would not exist. Think of music like water; it's built up of three crucial parts, two hydrogen and one oxygen. If you remove any one of those parts, the remaining two will turn into something completely different to what you had before.

Harmony and melody are both used to help describe the relationship between pitch in music without considering their duration. Rhythm exists to explain sounds and their duration without considering their pitch.

Harmony

Harmony is simply the product of combining notes together. By taking one note and adding other notes to it, and playing them at the same time or in a pattern, you've gone ahead and added a harmony to that original note. That is the easiest way to describe harmony to the uninitiated.

Harmony can be a very complex network of relationships between notes. It's a spider's web of interconnecting sounds. When you can grasp the relationship between two notes on a harmonic level, you start to see them as one moving structure rather than two separate entities.

In a sense, harmony is the driving force between music theory, it's the art and science of taking many moving musical parts and looking at them like one smooth running machine.

Melody

Melody can often be confused with harmony as they both are used to describe the relationship between pitches. But, while harmony is more about looking at music as a solid structure, melody is about looking at a note's individual qualities. Melody is all about describing the way notes work together in a sequence. If you were to take three separate notes, you would use melody to describe how they have different values depending on the order that you play them in, even if those three notes have the same harmonic value when played at the same time.

Melody and harmony work hand-in-hand in most pieces of music. Often melody is seen as a part of a larger harmony, a part that focuses on the way notes sound when played in a sequence one after the other. Normally musicians would add harmony to a melody, this provides a structure and foundation to the melody, or they may add a melody to an existing harmony to provide a focal point to a piece of music.

Rhythm

Rhythm is the timekeeper of music. This refers to the time between notes, intervals, and beats in music. Time, in music, is incredibly important. If you were to take a single note and play it continuously, you'd have a senseless drone, but if you periodically silence that note you suddenly have a rhythm. Rhythm is used to describe that pulse found in music, their pace, frequency, and the general on-off tendency that music has. Like melody and harmony, rhythm also has structures. These are used to define the way a piece of music moves and changes based on time divisions used by musicians. While obviously important, rhythm is a lesser focus in most music theory. It's ever present, but definitely the least complex of the three musical keystones.

Root Notes

The concept of a root note is very important in music. As we have already mentioned, music is built up from many different structures, and the root note is often the foundation of many of these structures.

The root note of a chord or scale is the note that is used to express the interval relationships of the rest of the notes in that scale and chord. The root note tends to be the lowest chord in a scale or chord. To put it simply, all of the notes in a scale or chord relate back to the root note and are defined by it.

When looking at chords and scales, you may notice a pattern. All of the names begin with a note, for example C Major scale or A minor chord. The root note is the note that the scale or chord is named after, so if you see a C Major 7th chord, you know that C is the root note of that chord and that the rest of the chord is defined based on that C. If someone is talking about an E Major scale, you know that E is the root note of that scale and the rest of the notes in that scale are defined based on that first E note.

SCALES AND MODES

What is a Scale?

Scales are incredibly important structures in music. They are used to describe almost all of the melodic and harmonic properties of a piece of music. They can be used to create chords and progressions, and can then be used to create melodies to be played over those chords and progressions. Musicians also use them to improvise and come up with music on the fly.

A scale is simply a grouping of notes which musicians can use to relate to other notes and pitches in a way which creates music. A scale doesn't necessarily have an order or a particular arrangement, it is just a collection of notes that work well together and have positive harmonic relationships.

We use the term "collection" to describe the notes in a scale because unlike a sequence, these notes do not have a specific order or place to be played. They can be played in any order and in any combination, they are just a set of notes that occupy a certain space on the musical spectrum.

Because of this, when using a scale it isn't necessary to play all of those notes. It also isn't necessary to play only those notes. Scales are designed to be mixed and matched with other scales and groupings. Think of each scale like a collection of letters from the alphabet, if you take a few collections and put them together, you may end up with a full word.

Scales are very abstract in this way, you have to make of them what you will. They don't have a set list of rules or instructions and therefore they can be some of the most powerful tools in a creative musician's arsenal.

To put into perspective just how flexible and general scales can be, you can play a B.B. King solo or a Pearl Jam solo, and they will both actually be using a minor pentatonic scale. Scales allow us to keep track of what someone else is doing musically, they act as a common reference point. Regardless of the genre, instrument, or type of composition, you can always spot what scale they are using and get a general idea of what is going on. You will also be able to figure out how it will sound if they suddenly play a certain collection of notes over that harmony.

Scales come in quite a few different forms; some have seven notes, some have five, some have many more than that. But, all of them have a root note that is the center of the melody and harmony, and all of them are built up from a set of relationships between all of the notes in that scale.

While scales are very fluid and up to interpretation, they all have a basic formula of tones and semitones. By knowing this scale formula, one can very easily figure out the notes of any scale and play them on nearly any instrument.

When it comes to chords, scales are used to define them. The harmonic structure of almost every piece of music is built up from chords, on top of this, the melody of most songs is also created from compatible scales. In most songs, the melody is a collection of single notes played over the chord-based harmony, this melody is created using either the same scale, or another compatible scale, that the harmony chords were created from. The chromatic scale is the best starting point for learning about scales, it is also known as the "master scale" due to its importance.

The Chromatic Scale

The father of all scales in western music is the chromatic scale. This scale contains all 12 tones, in every octave, and therefore it contains all other scales inside of it. Every single chord and scale is found inside of this scale.

Because this scale is so ridiculously large, it is often used to describe the entire harmonic layout of western music. Everything that is played, as long as it is tuned to standard, is related to everything else. The chromatic scale is the thing causing that relation, it is the canvas that the art of music is painted on. While most scales start in a particular Key, the chromatic scale is the source of all keys, and therefore, does not have one itself.

The chromatic scale, despite being incredibly important to western music, is very rarely used because of its abstract and musically inharmonious sound when played without any type of creative manipulation.

While the chromatic scale does cover every note, in every key, it is not something you want to use in composing or improvising, it's just too big.

We need to cut the chromatic scale up into bite-sized, more harmonious, groups of notes. We often want to define much smaller and more melodic spaces in the musical canvas for us to work off of. That is where all of the other smaller and more precise scales come into play.

The chromatic scale is made up of 12 notes per octave, this is then broken up into 12 semitones or six whole tones. These 12 notes are simply the notes from the note circle, in that very order.

While you won't often hear it in songs or compositions, it is incredibly easy to recite the chromatic scale and you'll often see it being used as a popular technical exercise by musicians. To play it, you need simply start on any note and play everything before or after it until you reach that same note and octave higher or lower.

Understanding all the scales in music is something that takes years to fully grasp. I can guarantee that many of your idols in music still haven't got a complete grasp of scales and their many uses. But don't let that stop you, all that does is show you the amazing amount of possibilities that music has to offer. Rather than dread the size of the musical landscape in front of me, I prefer to think about the cozy little corner I can carve out for myself.

The chromatic scale allows you to do anything you want, all you need is the knowledge to be able to pick out those little sections of it that are actually useful to you in the moment.

Types of Scales

We know that the chromatic scale is massive and all encompassing, but it may surprise you to learn that there are only a select few types of scales which we can pull from it.

In western music theory, there are two types of scales which make the building blocks of harmony, and those two scales further break up into a few other types.

Firstly, you have pentatonic scales. The "penta" stands for five, which is the number of notes in those scales. The various pentatonic scales are already enough to produce an incredible plethora of different harmonies and melodies in the musical landscape. While there are a few different note patterns which can create pentatonic scales, the most important and commonly used is the pattern which creates both the minor pentatonic and the Major pentatonic.

These two scales are most commonly found in blues and rock music, although they have been used in everything from jazz to pop music too. They are named minor and Major, because they originate from the seven note minor and Major scales.

Alongside your five note pentatonic scales, you have seven note scales. The fundamentals of which are known as diatonic scales. The most common of these are the Major scale (the stereotypical do-re-me) and the natural minor scale.

In regards to scales, the words minor and Major are used to describe the mood and feel of the scale. Major scales tend to sound more happy, lighter, and more progressive. Minor scales, on the other hand, tend to sound more melancholic, darker, and slower.

For those reasons, you will often see Major scales used in upbeat rock, country, or pop. While minor scales are much more suited to blues, metal, and other moodier genres of music.

There are two further variations of seven note scales which are often used in classical music, progressive rock, and jazz. These are the melodic minor scale and the harmonic minor scale.

Aside from the typical seven and five note scales, there are the eight note bebop scales used in jazz. In fact, jazz musicians are famed for creating many of their own scales by picking and choosing notes from the chromatic scale and placing them into seemingly random scales.

The Minor Pentatonic Scale

While you can build many types of pentatonic scales, there is only one which is commonly used in western music. This scale has two variations, the minor pentatonic and the major pentatonic.

The minor pentatonic is the most famous of the two, being the best friend to many blues, rock, metal, jazz, and bluegrass musicians. This scale is synonymous with being moody, emotional, and incredibly effective at telling a musical story.

The minor pentatonic scale has the added benefit of being one of the easiest scales to remember, and being very easy to compose with.

We use intervals to define scales and the intervals for the minor pentatonic scale are the first that any contemporary musician should learn.

The minor pentatonic scale is built up from five distinct notes. A root, a minor 3rd, a Perfect 4th, a Perfect 5th, and a minor 7th.

These numbers describe the notes position within the diatonic scale. But these intervals do exist inside many other scales too, including this one, the minor pentatonic. If you were to play the minor pentatonic scale in order, you would have something like this:

- You would start on the Root note.
- After the Root is a note a step and a half above it, this is a minor 3rd.

- Then comes a note a full step above that, this is the Perfect 4th.
- Following that, another full step up, this is the Perfect 5th.
- And lastly, a note a step and a half above that, the minor 7th.

You can visualize this scale in an easier way, like this:

W+H (1.5) - W (1) - W (1) - W+H (1.5) - W (1)

This, shown above, is called the scale formula. This formula is unique to most scales, and in this case it is for the minor pentatonic. The formula simply represents the pattern of intervals in a scale.

By only knowing the formula, you can take any 12 note instrument and play the scale as long as you know where your root is.

For example, if you were to start on an E note, you could play the E minor pentatonic by following the formula as such:

- E is the root.
- G is a step and a half above E, a minor 3rd.
- A is a step above G, a Perfect 4th.
- B is a step above A, a Perfect 5th.
- D is a step and a half above B, minor 7th.
- E is a step above D, a full Octave above the root.

If you place the root of this scale on the root of a chord, then pretty much every note in the scale will sound good when played over that chord. That makes this scale particularly good for improvising. As long as you know the root chord of a progression, you can play the minor pentatonic on that root over it.

What Is a Mode?

Now that we're familiar with the minor pentatonic scale, let's use it to demonstrate another important concept in musical theory. We know that the minor pentatonic scale is made up of five notes, and that when they are based around a root note, they are then defined by a particular set of intervals.

What if we take those same notes, in this example let's use the notes of the A minor pentatonic scale (A, C, D, E, and G), and move them around. Instead of calling A the root note, let's take these same notes and rather call C the root, this will make it a C scale.

This means that the notes will now have different names:

- C is now a Root note and no longer a minor 3rd.
- D is now a Major 2nd and no longer a Perfect 4th.
- E is now a Major 3rd.
- G is now a Perfect 5th.
- A is now a Major 6th.

This makes the new scale; a Root, Major 2nd, Major 3rd, Perfect 5th, and Major 6th. This is a totally different collection of note definitions than the A minor pentatonic scale that we started with, even though we technically are still using the same notes. The reason for this change is because we are now using a different set of intervals.

Using the same pattern, but beginning on a different note creates a new scale. In the above example, that scale is the C Major pentatonic scale, another very common and popular scale in modern music.

By moving the Root of the scale, we have created something commonly referred to as a mode. You can actually say that the Major pentatonic scale is a mode of the minor pentatonic scale, or vice versa.

Like the minor pentatonic, the Major pentatonic scale is also very popular and is commonly seen across country and pop music. The Major pentatonic has a much happier and lighter sound than that of its minor counterpart, this is due to all of its notes being a part of the Major scale.

With each of the five notes in the minor pentatonic scale, there is potential for a mode to be played from that note. You simply need to take the interval pattern used in the minor pentatonic, and start playing that same pattern on the next note in the scale. Continue that through all five notes, and you will find yourself with five different modes, all of whom sound completely different.

Keys and Signatures

We've mentioned keys a few times so far in this book, but without much explanation as to what they are and their importance in music. Lets go ahead and change that right now!

In pretty much every situation, a song or composition is built around some form of scale. This is usually the major or minor scale which has a root note as its center. The root note in this instance is often known as the key of a piece. Usually you'll see this key written as a note followed by Major or minor, for example "F minor" or "C# Major". Because there are 12 notes, that means that we have 12 possible keys for us to use.

The key to a piece of music acts as the harmonic center. By knowing the key, a musician immediately gains some key knowledge about the song, mainly the scale which is used. When it comes to most rock, blues, and pop songs, knowing the key is all you'll often need to know which notes will sound good being improvised over the song.

In jazz and more avant-garde genres, it can be much more complex than that. The songs in these genres often traverse various harmonic centers as the song is played, meaning different scales need to be played at different points. Although, most of the time the key of a song is the foundation that every musician needs to start analyzing a song and it's harmonic structure.

When a musician writes a song, whether they know it or not, they always point out what scale the song is built around. A key will tell us how many flat and sharp notes are found inside of that scale. For example, C Major has absolutely no sharps or flats in it, but E Major has four sharps: F#, G#, C#, and D#. This number of sharp or flat notes in a key is known as the key signature.

The Circle of Fifths and Fourths

I know when I started learning musical theory, one of the first things my theory teacher gave me was a piece of paper with a circle drawn onto it. This circle was surrounded by a bunch of notes, and to be honest I had no idea what it was. At the time, I kept that to myself though, I didn't want to look like a complete illiterate in front of my teacher. Soon enough though, it became apparent that I had no idea what I was doing, and my teacher had to explain to me what this strange circle was, and why it was arguably the most important diagram in music.

That circle is known as the circle of fifths. It is a tool we used to visualize arranging notes into intervals of Perfect fifths. This is useful for a whole load of reasons; it helps to show us relationships of all the possible notes you can play, it allows us to get a better grasp of chord progressions, and it also marks some important features for each key that help us understand their internal structures.

Most importantly though, the circle of fifths gives you a simple way to remember how many sharps and flats are in each diatonic key.

Starting on C Major, which has no sharps or flats, you can move up or down the circle by fifth intervals to find out what other keys will look like and what their key signatures will be. A circle of fifths simply shows you what all the keys look like when arranged in intervals of fifths.

A fifth above C is G, a fifth above that is D, then A, followed by E, next comes B, and finally F#. With every move we make down the right side of the circle, we add a sharp onto the note that is specified. C has no sharps, G has one, D has two, E has three, and so on.

F# sits at the base of the circle, and while we could travel the entire way clockwise around until we reach C at the top again, we typically don't. Usually you will travel from C down the right hand side of the circle to F#, or from C down the left hand side of the circle to Gb (F#) at the base.

When you descend counterclockwise on the circle of fifths, the notes become lower in pitch by a perfect fifth with each interval. If you ascend counterclockwise on the circle of fifths that is considered the circle of fourths, a reflection of the circle of fifths. It is exactly the same as the circle of fifths in structure, the only difference is that the notes gain pitch as you travel around the circle.

The relationship between notes, by a fifth interval, is often considered one of the key building blocks of harmony. By marking the notes in ascending or descending fifths, a method is created in which all notes are represented and displayed easily.

That method, shown as a circle, helps to tell us things about these notes when we use them to create keys, for example, the structure of those keys. The best thing about this method though, is that it very clearly shows how keys relate to each other and work together.

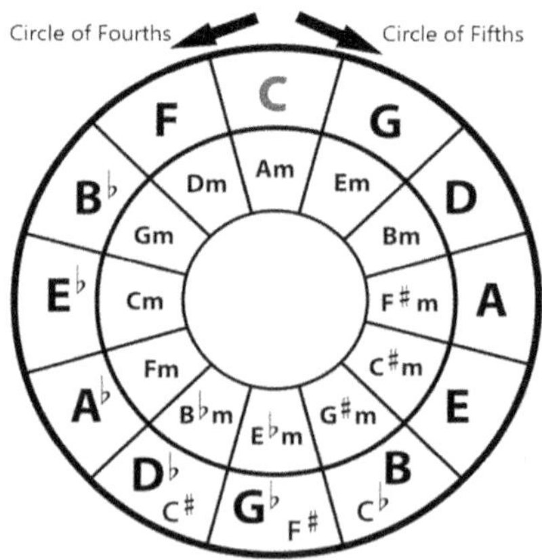

MASTERING CHORDS

What is a Chord?

While some instruments are designed to only play one note at a time, there are some instruments which can play a combination of notes together. Guitars and pianos are the best known of these instruments and can include upwards of three notes in their chords.

A chord, in its most simple form, is a grouping of two or more notes being played in unison with each other. This also means a chord is the sound that is produced when we combine the sounds of any two or more notes together at the same time.

Chords are created using scales, in fact, they are made up from the specific notes used in scales. Each scale has its own list of chords, and once a musician has a scale in mind, they should then be able to pull chords from the notes in that scale.

Much like scales, chords are based around a root note. This root note is also what decides the name of a chord, which in turn also tells us which notes are inside of that chord. The name will tell us exactly which root the chord is built on and which intervals that chord is created from.

The interval structure of a chord is known as the 'spelling' of that chord, and if you know the name of a chord, then you'll be able to figure out which notes are contained within it.

For example, if we were to take a Major 7th chord and deconstruct it, we will find that it is created from a Root, a Major 3rd, and Perfect 5th, and a Major 7th note.

These notes make up the spelling of the chord. If we then go and specify a root note, like G, that chord then becomes a G Major 7th. Now take those intervals and place them over a G Major scale, you will see that those intervals align with these notes on the scale: G, B, D, and F#.

How Are They Built?

Typically, chords are created from intervals of thirds. This means that they are created from a root and notes that ascend above the root in a series of thirds. To make this structure, all you need to do is take a scale and count upwards in thirds from a root note. So in other words, you count up two degrees at a time in the scale to reach notes that you will use in your chords.

In a similar fashion to scales, chords can be explained by their chord formulas. Because chords are created from notes in a scale, their formula is built off of the scale degrees from its parent scale. If we take the formula the Major 7th chord used above (1, 3, 5, 7), it means that this chord is made up from the first scale degree, the third, fifth, and seventh. Now, if we take the Major scale and assign it a root note, we can apply this pattern over it to get the Major 7th chord for that scale.

Chord Types

Any sound produced by more than one note falls under the definition of a chord. That means that any time you hear multiple notes played at once, a chord has been formed. We classify chords according to the amount of notes that they use, and while it is technically possible to have up to 12 notes in a chord, the typical formations have two, three, or four notes. In some jazz and classical compositions you may see notes with more than four notes, but these are generally less common and are usually an extended version of a three or four note chord.

Most of the time, chords are created from three or four notes, although it is very common to see a note repeated in a chord on another octave. This means that we can have more than three or four tones creating that chord. If you take one of the most basic beginner guitar notes, the E minor, you will notice that although you play all six strings, there are only three distinct notes being used. The rest are repeated notes on different octaves that act to make the chord sound larger and more full.

The most common chords that you will run into are three note chords called triads. In more complicated harmonies you will also run into four note chords called 7th chords or quads.

Overall, the most common forms of chords are:

- Dyads - Two note chords.
- Triads - Three note chords.
- Quads - Four note chords.

In regards to triads and quads, these notes are almost always built upon the system of thirds that we talked about earlier, these are known as stacked thirds.

In regards to dyads though, any interval can be used. Any chromatic interval can be a dyad chord, this means that you can get Major, minor, Perfect, diminished, and augmented dyads. The most common dyads that you will hear are in rock and are created by playing two notes which are a fifth apart. These chords consist of a Root and a Perfect 5th, and are commonly known as "power chords".

Triad Chords

Three note chords are the easiest to understand and use in songs, therefore we will make this our starting point for wading into chords. Remember, when we refer to triads, we are almost always talking about chords that are composed of three notes, two thirds stacked upon each other over a Root note.

Below are the different types of triad chords:

- Major triads: These chords are built up from a Root, a Major 3rd, and a minor 3rd. This is your most common triad, a simple Root with a Major 3rd above that and a Perfect fifth on top of that. The formula for this chord is 1 - 3 - 5.
- Minor triads: These chords are built up from a Root, a minor 3rd and a Major 3rd stacked atop each other. This

means that minor triads consist of a Root, and minor 3rd, and a Perfect 5th. You will notice that this is the inverse of the Major triad. In terms of the formula for this chord, you have the Root (1), then a minor 3rd instead of a Major 3rd. This means that we have to flatten our interval down one semitone, so our 3 becomes a b3. Lastly, we have a normal Perfect 5th. This means that a minor triad formula is simply 1 - b3- 5. It's amazing how only flattening the middle note by one semitone can change a chord from something that sounds bright and happy, into something darker and more emotional. This just goes to show that the 3rd interval used in chords is incredibly important to the overall feel of the chord.

- Augmented triads: These are simply Major triads with a sharpened 5th. This means that they are constructed using two Major 3rds stacked atop each other. These chords contain a Root, a Major 3rd, and an augmented 5th. The sound these chords produce is very dissonant and uncomforting, so they are rarely the focal point of a piece. But, because of their interesting feel, they are often used to contrast happy sounds and add emotion. The formula for an augmented triad is 1 - 3 - #5. The #5 lets us know that we only need to raise our Perfect 5th by one semitone.

- Diminished triads: These chords are minor triads with a flat 5th. Rather than having the minor 3rd and the Major 3rd of a minor triad, these have two minor thirds stacked atop each other. This means they consist of a Root, a minor 3rd, and a diminished 5th. The formula for diminished triads is 1 - b3 - b5, which shows that both the 3rd and 5th notes are flattened.

Quad Chords

Slightly more complicated than triads, quad chords have an extra fourth note added into the equation. While triads have two 3rds, quad chords have a third 3rd note added to their formula, this is usually in the form of a 7th note.

Although they are rather similar to triads, quads are built in a larger variety of ways and have a larger variety of combinations because of the extra note. Although, they are all generally some version of a 7th chord, which is created with a Root, a 3rd, a 5th, and a 7th.

Due to the greater number of notes, quad harmonies can be much more complex and difficult to play around. There are more notes clashing and less room to fit general melodies into the mix.

Below are the different types of quad chords:

- Major 7th: These chords are built up from a Major 3rd interval, with a minor 3rd, and another Major 3rd atop it. This means that they feature a Root, a Major 3rd, a Perfect 5th, and a Major 7th. The formula for these chords is 1 - 3 - 5 - 7.
- Minor 7th: These chords are created with a minor 3rd, with a Major 3rd, and another minor 3rd atop it. They follow the typical inverse structure that minors follow compared to Major. This means that they feature a Root, a minor 3rd, a Perfect 5th, and a minor 7th. The formula for these chords is 1 - b3 - 5 - b7.
- Dominant 7th: These chords form a middle ground between the Major and minor 7th chords. They have a Root, a Major 3rd, a Perfect 5th, and a minor 7th. This means they feature a Major 3rd followed by two minor 3rds. Although they may seem very similar to the two previously mentioned chords, they sound completely different and occupy a vastly different use in music. While the previous two are commonly used for their amazing harmonic abilities, these chords are very dissonant and are typically only used to build tension. The formula for these chords is 1 - 3 - 5 - b7.
- Minor 7b5: The name given to these chords may come across as pretty intimidating at first, but they're actually just a minor 7th with a flat 5th note shoved in. These chords are built up from a Root, a minor 3rd, a diminished 5th, and a

minor 7th. This means that they consist of a minor 3rd interval, with another minor 3rd, and a major 3rd atop that. You'll know these chords as soon as you hear them due to their very unique 'jazzy' sound. The formula for minor 7b5 chords is 1 - b3 - b5 - b7

- Diminished 7th: Also known as full diminished chords, these chords take the 7th chord sound to extremes. They are created with only a stack of minor 3rd intervals, which is where they get their other name, symmetrical chords. Their interval structure stays the same, regardless of whether you are increasing or decreasing pitch. Jazz musicians love to use these chords to fill the gaps and create transitions between keys. They sound dark, unnerving, and even as if the musician made a mistake, but they are very useful for creating occasional drama in a piece. They are built from a Root, a minor 3rd, a diminished 5th, and a Major 6th. This means their formula is 1 - b3 - b5 - bb7.

- Major 6th: These chords are one of the best known sounds in Jazz and have a very cool, interesting sound. They are often thrown into a usual triad progression to add a bit of flavor. They are created with a Major 3rd, a minor 3rd, and a Major 2nd interval. This means that they have a Root, a Major 3rd, a Perfect 5th, and a Major 6th. Their formula is 1 - 3 - 5 - 6.

- Minor 6th: Lastly, we have the minor 6th. These quads are the same as a Major 6th chord, except they have a minor 3rd note. They are built up from a minor 3rd, a Major 3rd, and a Major 2nd. This means they contain a Root, a minor 3rd, a Perfect 5th, and a Major 6th. Their formula is 1 - b3 - 5 - 6.

How Do Chords Come From Scales?

As we've already mentioned, chords come from scales. They are created by taking the notes in a scale, in a certain pattern, and playing them at the same time. This means that a certain scale will give you a certain list of chords that can be played from it, which are all in the same key as the scale.

Chords that come from diatonic (Major) scales are always known as diatonic chords. Every Major scale key has its own individual set of seven potential chords, with each chord being rooted on a different scale note.

Figuring out the chords in a major key is a pretty simple undertaking. For example, say you want to figure out all the chords that are found in the key of C major. Firstly, we want to take the C Major scale and assign a number to each note on the scale, let's go a little bit above an octave. Something like this C (1), D (2), E (3), F (4), G (5), A (6), B (7), C (8), D (9), E (10), F (11), G (12), A (13).

We know by now that chords are usually built in thirds, so let's simply start by stacking thirds on top of each other. Take C (1) and add E (3) and G (5) to it.

This results in a simple triad chord. If you were to do that for every scale degree, you would end up getting seven different sets of three notes. You can then analyze those notes and figure out which chords they create. For example, we know we have a C Major if we take the C, E, G chord above. If we move this up a scale degree so that the notes are D (2), F (4), and A (6), we then get a D minor chord.

Transposing

One of the most overlooked, yet important, skills any musician can have is the ability to transpose chords. This allows you to have total flexibility in your playing, being able to take any series of chords and move it up and down in scale degrees as you need.

When playing with a singer, you often need to make sure that you can play in a key which frames and supports their voice well, this can mean needing to raise or lower the key of a song.

Luckily, because we already know the patterns used for producing chords in the Major scale, we can figure this out pretty easily. If we have a sequence of chords playing and we want to switch to another key we can do it through a simple method. For example, if you have this progression C (1) - Am (6) - F (4) - G (5), in order to switch that C Major progression to one in G Major, you would need to figure out the chords in the key of G and use that same progression.

The notes in the G Major scale are: G, A, B, C, D, E, F#.

If you take the intervals of the Major scale: 1 (Major), 2 (minor), 3 (minor), 4 (Major), 5 (Major), 6 (minor), 7 (diminished). And then apply them to the notes of the G Major scale, you get the following chords G Major, A minor, B minor, C Major, D Major, E minor, F# diminished.

All you then need to do is take that 1 - 6 - 4 - 5 pattern and apply it to those chords to get the following progression: G - Em - C - D. The progression that was previously in the key of C has now easily been transposed in the key of G.

WHY IS RHYTHM IMPORTANT

The Fundamentals of Rhythm

Rhythm is undoubtedly one of the most important things in music. It is almost impossible to make something sound bad, provided you have a bit of rhythm, groove, or mojo.

Ask any jazz, blues, or soul musician and they'll tell you exactly that, you don't need to be a great player as long as you can play with rhythm.

But, developing a good rhythm is far more than just being able to read and piece together notes and numbers. Rhythm is something that comes from spending a lot of time with your instrument and the type of music you want to play, it comes from comfort, developing your own style of play, and creating an internal metronome.

I know from personal experience that it can be incredibly difficult to develop some of these rhythmic tools. The best ways that I've found to improve your rhythm are by playing with other musicians, playing along to recordings of yourself, or using backing tracks.

As long as you focus on playing slow, with clean notes and good timing, you'll certainly improve. A big mistake many newcomers make is trying to go into this with speed, rhythm isn't about speed at all, it's all about being in the groove.

By playing slowly, you force yourself to focus on your timing and the way you play in relation to the rhythm of the piece you're playing along to.

And, as you improve, you will notice that you'll be able to play faster without falling out of rhythm. That's the key, any fast playing always starts out as slow and repeated practise.

With all of this in mind, let's get into the fundamental elements of rhythm, the key parts to sounding like you know what you're doing as a musician.

Time, Beat, Tempo, and Bar.

In terms of music theory, time is used to refer to the beat of a song and it's time signature. The beat is the most important unit of time in music and is the same thing that we always end up tapping our foot to while listening to a catchy song. Overall, the time signature of a piece defines the time present in the rhythm.

Tempo helps to describe the rate which beats happen at in a piece of music. This unit is often notated in beats per minute or BPM. The tempo is the pulse of a song in many ways, not just in its similar unit of measurement, but also in the fact that without it, there would be no life to that music.

If you can figure out the timing and tempo of a piece, you will know how to then play over it. The timing and tempo set the tone, make the mood apparent, and help musicians understand the overall vibe of a piece of music. It is possible to go into a piece, knowing nothing at all about it, but still being able to improvise over it by knowing the timings at which you should play and tempo which you should follow.

Time Divisions

One of the most important aspects of music theory, and most perplexing to newcomers, is the concept of time divisions. Music relies heavily on mathematics in the way that beats and notes are divided into values. As a natural part of music, notes get played and held for certain amounts of time, these notes are given numerical values to express that.

In western music theory, the following note values are commonly seen:

- Whole Notes (Semibreve): A note which is held for the entire length of a common bar.
- Half Notes (Minim): A note held for half the length of the whole note.

- Quarter Notes (Crotchet): A note held for a quarter of a whole note, or half of a half note.
- Eighth Notes (Quaver): A note held for an eighth of a whole note, or half a quarter note.
- Sixteenth Notes (Semiquaver): A note held for a sixteenth of a whole note, or half an eighth note.
- Thirty-Second Notes (Demisemiquaver): A note held for a thirty-second of a whole note, or a half of a sixteenth note.

These notes are considered the most common in western music and will often be seen scattered about most pieces of music.

There are some rarer longer notes which do occasionally see use too, these are:

- Double Whole Notes (breve): A note that is held for two bars.
- Longa: A note that is held for four bars.
- Maxima: A note that is held for eight bars.
- Finally, there are also some notes which are shorter than the thirty-second note. These notes are very rarely seen and typically only pop-up in very fast runs:
- Sixty-Fourth Notes (Hemidemisemiquavers): A note held for a half of a thirty-second note.
- One Hundred Twenty-Eighth Notes (Semihemidemisemiquavers): A note held for a half of a sixty-fourth note.
- Two Hundred Fifty-Sixth Notes (Demisemihemidemisemiquavers): A note held for a half of a one hundred twenty-eighth note.

It may sound a bit confusing, but it is completely possible to play very short notes, like thirty-second and sixteenth notes, which sound very fast paced while still keeping a slow tempo. One can also only play a few long notes, such as whole notes and half notes, even if the tempo of a song is very fast. For both of these cases, the tempo of the song is what decides the feeling of speed in the song.

Think of it this way, if you need to walk 20 feet you can do that in a few large leaps or a multitude of small steps, but depending on how quickly you do those actions you can still arrive at your destination in the same amount of time.

If all of this wasn't complicated enough, the simple divisions above can all be augmented with a small dot next to them. This dot means that they become a dotted note which causes the note to become 1.5 times the length of its usual value. Some examples of this are:

- A dotted whole note equals one whole note plus one half note.
- A dotted half note equals one half note plus one quarter note.
- A dotted quarter note equals one quarter note plus one eighth note.
- A dotted eighth note equals one eighth note plus one sixteenth note.
- A dotted sixteenth note equals one sixteenth note plus one thirty-second note.

Time Signatures

Time signatures make up the underlying backbone of all musical pieces, these decide the structure of a bar of music. They act to tell us the number of beats that fit into a bar and the value assigned to each note in that bar. Alongside telling us the tempo of a piece of music, the time signature acts as an indication of the rhythm that a song may have, which as we've already addressed is very important.

As we've already seen, time in music is shown in ratios, and that is no different for time signatures. They are directly connected to the note division ratios that we have already talked about. You'll see the time signature of a piece of sheet music shown at the beginning of the musical staff, it is displayed as two numbers, one on top of the other.

In modern music, we have a signature known as common time, this is 4/4.

The top number in the musical ratio indicates the number of divided notes that can fit into the bar. This does not tell you how many notes are in the bar, rather how many can actually fit in. So, in 4/4 this means that four notes can fit into each bar.

The second number represents the note value of the notes in the bar. This number can only be 2, 4, 8, 16, 32, and so on. Knowing this number means the performer can understand the pace of a song. In 4/4, the performer knows that each bar can contain four quarter notes.

Polymeters and Polyrhythms

By using a bit of musical math and creativity, it is possible to create some very complex and rhythmic time signatures. A composer can move between multiple signatures in one song which makes it possible to create some incredibly dense and intricate rhythmic structures in music.

It is also worth keeping in mind that separate time signatures can be placed on top of each other, either by the same musician or by different members of a band.

This is what we refer to as a polyrhythm or a polymeter. This is, of course, a rather advanced concept and not something I would throw a beginner into just yet.

It is important though to understand the role this concept plays in rhythmic structure.

Polyrhythms are two bars of the same size being played on top of each other that have different time signatures. For example, a musician may play a bar of 4/4 and a bar of 8/4 over each other.

Polymeters function by mixing two different time signatures so that the length of each pulse is the same. This makes it so that bars of different sizes are able to complement each other and play in and out of time as a song progresses.

You'll most commonly see these concepts used in Metal, progressive rock, classical music, jazz, and avant garde forms of improvisation.

Dynamics, Accents, Tempo Changes, and Syncopations

Once you have a grasp of the timing of a piece of music, you then need to know how to play along to it. It's pretty hard to make interesting things happen if all you're doing is playing to the exact same pulse and rhythm as the music. Most musicians will intentionally miss notes, play off-beat, and skip over beats to create surprising changes in the otherwise predictable fabric of a song. This is where syncopation becomes a key part of your musical repertoire.

Syncopation is simply the act of playing in the empty spaces between a song's rhythm. Playing longer and shorter notes, skipping beats, taking rests, and changing tempo are all different examples of using syncopation to add some excitement to a piece. Syncopation is all about taking a well structured rhythm and adding a bit of imperfect groove to it.

To add to that, players can add accents to a song to add more variety to their syncopation and variation. By adding or reducing speed or volume, a performer can suddenly ramp up or cut down intensity and drama in a song. You can do this either by throwing in more notes, which makes the song sound faster, or by slowing down the rate at which you play the already existing notes.

Another key way of producing more personality in a piece is through the usage of dynamics in improvisation. A performer can hammer down the dark parts of a song by playing dissonant notes where they otherwise wouldn't. Similarly, a performer can bring life back into a song by slipping bright diatonic sounds into areas of otherwise anxious or dark music. This is a very common practise in blues, jazz, and funk.

MOVEMENT IN MUSIC

Dynamics

Dynamics are some of the most important basic elements of music. When we talk about a dynamic in musical theory, it's a fancy term for the volume of a sound. To be a bit more in depth, it's the volume *and* how that volume is approached (is it sudden and violent, is it a slow rise, etc.).

The movement associated with the dynamics of a piece of music are a major force behind the drama and emotion in that music. A composition getting louder or softer, elongating or shortening sounds, and providing sudden rises or drops, can all contribute massively to how that piece of music is perceived by the listener.

Regardless of the genre, musicians of all backgrounds need to be able to manipulate and play with the dynamics of a song in order to produce emotion and movement.

This is arguably the most simple tool at our disposal, but undoubtedly one of the most potent ways of turning otherwise emotionless music into something bursting with drama, tension, sadness, anger, and a multitude of other feelings important to the listener.

Timbre and Tone

While the dynamics deal with the volume of a noise and its delivery, the timbre (or tone) of a note refers to the color of a note.

What is the color of a note, you ask? Well, to put it simply, it's the quality of a note, it's the way a sound sounds. Think about it this way, if you play an E note on a guitar, that will sound vastly different compared to the E note played on a trombone.

While these are technically the same notes, with the same frequencies, the instrument itself and the way it is played makes it sound different. This is the timbre.

The terms tone and timbre are often used interchangeably, and while this often is fine, there is a slight difference between them.

We already know what the timbre is, but what is the tone? The tone relates to the tonal quality of an instrument based on factors like its inherent acoustics, the playing technique used, the form of sound amplification, and any external effects that may be applied to it.

Tone tends to refer to the instrument and the sounds it produces, while timbre is specific to the qualities of a sound.

Dissonance and Consonance

Dissonance and consonance are two fundamental elements to moving any piece of music. Through these two elements we can create chaos and uncertainty or direction and resolution.

We tend to want music to sound good at all times, but often for that to happen, we need dissonant sounds for that to contrast against. Consonant sound, pleasant music that feels like it has direction and leads towards a resolution, is only as distinct as the dissonant sounds it contrasts to.

Consonant sounds exist to calm listeners, to provide them with a release of tension and anxiety in music. While, on the other hand, dissonant sounds exist to create that tension and anxiety.

Think of consonants as notes that feel like they belong between the notes around them. Dissonants rather wedge themselves into spaces where they don't sound like they belong in the harmony.

By using dissonant and consonant ideas in music, alongside dynamics, tone, and timbre, a musician can build incredible tension in a piece in an instant, and cause it to wash away almost immediately after.

Drama

As we have stated earlier in this book, music is a language. Every composition is a story, and what story is complete without drama? In a musical sense, drama can be classified as the overall highs and lows of a piece of music.

Whether a song rises or falls, has climaxes or sudden periods of peace, parts high in anxiety or areas of harmonious flow, or any other forms of eclectic movement, all comes down to the drama of the music.

For a great musician, it is natural to use every tool at their disposal to create drama in music, even if these tools aren't strictly conventional. One can stay level on melody and harmony while still creating movements in a piece using clever note selections, manipulating harmonic materials, and changing harmonic structures (improvisation).

Alongside using the larger forms of harmony and melody to create drama, all of the other techniques for creating movement listed above, can be used in one way or another to increase the drama in a song. Overall, drama can be used as a bit of a blanket term for creating a sense of story with the tools available to a musician.

Creative Techniques

Keep in mind though, that music is an infinite realm of possibility. This means that there is always some way of creating movement in a piece of music. There are always ways of creating drama and emotion that go beyond the conventional, written techniques.

I've seen some incredibly talented acoustic guitarists use their guitars for drumming and scratching along with the more conventional uses for the instrument. I've seen trumpeters speak, shout, and whisper into their instruments. I've witnessed violinists place objects over their strings to create unique tones. Even the tremolo bar found on

many guitars can be considered an extended way of creating movement outside of the usual confines of the instrument.

While there are plenty of contemporary musicians that you may see
adopt these unusual techniques on occasion, you'll see them exten-
sively used throughout more avant-garde and experimental genres.
Regardless of what instrument you play, understanding creative
techniques like these allows you even further avenues into telling the
story that your music wants to tell.

HOW TO BUILD MUSICAL STRUCTURES

The first true move we can make towards building a mastery of musical theory is learning how to take the fundamentals of music, the theoretical structures we have talked about, and the concepts of musical theory, and put them together into a system which makes music. What we have talked about so far in this book is only enough to give you a basic understanding of what makes music, not how to make music, or how it actually works. Understanding and creating music is a lot more than just recognizing the basic elements of it. Music is a moving and breathing thing, and just like a doctor needs to know more than basic anatomy to operate, we need to know the nitty-gritty details of music before we can get started.

The end-game for any hopeful musician is more than just knowing how to make chords or play scales. It is mastery of every aspect of music, which comes from an understanding of musical structures, knowing how to put them to work, and manipulating them however you like. This is definitely not easy though, before you can dive in head first, it is necessary to have a basic introduction first.

A basic introduction to this subject will need to cover two things. Firstly, an explanation of the foundations of musical theory, which we have covered up until now. The second, is an explanation of how to put all of those separate structures together in order to sound like something which resembles music.

That second point is what we are hoping to cover from this point onwards. This chapter, in particular, exists to help you get on your feet and excited for the journey ahead of you. Here we will be explaining how musical elements, structures, and systems interact and work together to create songs. This section will set you up for that end goal, total mastery of the musical realm.

Explaining Composition

So, what is composition exactly? While music is an auditory art, it is very much structured on paper. Practising musicians tend to forget that music relies on written material almost as much as writing does.

Composition is more than just a creative person with a pen, paper, and basic understanding of chords. To compose is to intentionally create music, yes, but it is also so much more than that.

Firstly, you will find that there is non-compositional music. This is music which, although created intentionally, is not meant to be repeated. Secondly, you will find that there is sound which is created intentionally, like the sound of a whistle blowing, which we would never call music but is meant to be repeated. This means that composition is music that is meant to be repeated but is more than just a simple repeatable sound.

Compositions are meant to be repeatable, you are meant to be able to play it the same way each time. This is what separates a composer from an improviser. To add to that, music is more than just sound because of musical theory. Music is sound with structure, it is organized and timed. When you refer to the organization of sound, we are referring to musical structures like harmony, melody, and rhythm. These are the elements that musicians create and manipulate intentionally. A composer creates organization from sound and builds structure with the elements of music.

That is what composition is, it is the act of intentionally creating repeatable, controllable musical structures from the basic elements of sound.

The Relationship Between Improvisation and Composition

We've talked about composition being the intentional creation of musical structures, so what is improvisation then? At the end of the day, improvisation and composition should be thought of as two aspects of the same thing. Improvisation is just instantaneous composition. Instead of sitting at a desk writing music, you are on a stage writing it as you play. Sure, the stakes are higher, but if you have complete confidence in your knowledge, then there really isn't any difference.

Improvisation tends to reject many of the structures that have been set in place by traditional composition over the centuries. Composition is all about theoretical analysis, it's about writing down music, analysing it, and seeing where it can be improved. Improvisation, on the other hand, is all about making an intentionally imperfect and unanalyzed piece of music based solely on your ear and feel for the song. It's not like improvised music doesn't have harmony, melody, or rhythm, it just uses those elements in a different way to traditional composition.

A composer has all the time in the world to create music, time to test things out, analyze sounds, rearrange notes, and fiddle with timings. This changes the way a composer looks at musical theory, composers can spend as much time as they need to create music. At the end of a composition, a composer will have something far more rich and complete than an improviser could come up with on the spot.

Improvisers, obviously, don't have time. They are creating music based off of a split second snapshot of a song that they are currently hearing. It is not possible for them to stop and study a song, they can't rearrange or change anything. They have to take what they have at hand, and in one chance they have to create something from it.

Because of this, improvisers use shortcuts, cheats, and mnemonic methods to allow them to craft things on the spot. A good improviser is one that has memorized a handful of structures, themes, and devices that they can pull out at a moment's notice and apply to whatever they are hearing. Improvisers can take these tools and apply, manipulate, and combine them instantly to create something from nothing. In all honesty, improvisation is just the art of memorizing theory behind the scenes. That's really all it comes down to, it's knowing the shortcuts and cheat codes in normal musical theory that will allow you to improvise over anything. Improvisation is all about knowledge, experience, and a good memory.

Notes Relative to Other Notes

An important intermediate subject to understand in music is that of note relativism. An E is so much more than just a tone played at a certain pitch. In music, the absolute tone of a note is far less important than its relative value. That means that an E may be different depending on the context in which it is played in. It is possible for the same note to play different functions even though the sound itself does not change. What makes a note is its function and not its definition. While we may write a note the same way each time, what matters is how it's played and the context of its use, that is what makes music. Note relativism is simply our way of expressing what a note really is, it is an element that relies on other notes to make sense or sound good, the value of notes is always relative because of that.

For example, let's say you are playing a song in the key of E minor. If you play an A minor chord, that A Root note is fulfilling multiple jobs. It is the first note of its chord, it is the bass note of its chord, and it is the fourth note of the E minor scale. All of those things help to define and value the A note when it is played in that context.

Now imagine you are playing in Bb Major. If you play a Dm7 chord, there is still an A note in that chord, but now it is the fifth note in the chord you are playing, it is not the bass note in that chord, and it is only the seventh note in the Bb Major scale. While it is still fundamentally the same note as before, it is entirely different in this context because its function in this musical structure is completely different.

What we can see here is that notes are completely relative to the environment that they are featured in. This is one of the primary rules of harmony, that the importance of knowing when to play notes often beats playing the mathematically correct notes.

Musical theory is not a structure of immovable parts, it is not a tower of cards that can't be touched without falling over. While this is one of the best things about musical theory, it's also one of the things that makes it incredibly difficult to learn. It's easy to learn a solid set of rules, but as soon as those rules start changing and moving around then it becomes far more difficult to keep track. To study music theory is madness, it's like trying to photograph something that is invisible. Music is naturally fluid and ever-changing, and adding structure to that seems pointless at times, but it must be done in order for us to ever hope to make art from it.

By learning and accepting the fluid nature of music, you can slowly start to change the way you view musical theory. Up until now it has been compared to a science, and although it can be that on the surface, it is actually the most decentralized and fluid art form in existence.

How Do Chords Function in a Key?

Every key in there is seven basic chords. Each of these chords has a unique function. Although, for all seven of them there are only three general functions, these are basic functions that define the chords in a very broad sense, the three basic groups are: tonic, dominant, and subdominant.

Tonic chords are the most prominent and help to establish the key that they are played in. These are the chords that progressions naturally move to in order to release tension in the song. They are always the first, third, and sixth degrees of a scale.

Dominant chords are the tension builders in every progression, they naturally want to gravitate towards tonic chords which help to resolve their dissonant sound. These chords are the furthest chords away from tonic chords on the harmonic landscape which means that you typically want to turn around and travel back to a tonic chord once you reach them. Therefore, their main function is to lead a progression back towards its harmonic centre. They are always the fifth and seventh degrees in a scale and any chords created on those degrees.

Subdominant chords are the chords which act as a middleman between the tonic and dominant. They act as the method of moving a song away from its harmonic center towards the dissonant sounds of the dominant chord. They also then help carry the song back to its center when it leaves the dominant chord. While a tonic chord helps to establish the key, the subdominant acts as a slightly dissonant sound which threatens to build tension and drag a song away from that key. Subdominant chords don't always travel between tonic and dominant though, they can change directions and move back towards tonic chords before reaching dominant. These are always the second and fourth degrees on a scale.

For example, take the key of C. In C Major, a chord built using the C Major, E minor, or A minor triads is considered a tonic chord. All of these chords will help to define the key center.

Any chord that is constructed using the D minor or F Major triads will move away from the C Major tonic. These are our subdominant chords in this context, and they fill the second and fourth degrees in this scale.

Lastly, any chord built using the G Major or B diminished triads are dominant in nature. They will always be the fifth and seventh degrees of the scale and will act to create drama in a song. They will also act to turn the song around and bring it back to a place of resolution.

How Do Notes Function in a Chord?

The notes of a chord function are just as predictable in their functions as chords in a key. The most stable part of any chord is the triad, the notes between the first and fifth notes being the best sounding. This is why you can play nothing but a first and fifth note, a power chord, and sound great. These notes are the most consonant in a chord.

The third note is also stable but not nearly as much as the first and fifth. The three does, however, act to help determine if a chord is Major or minor.

When extending a triad, the first note you'd add is a seventh. This is, therefore, the next most stable note. This note acts as a means of adding color to a chord and deciding whether it is Major, minor, or dominant.

Finally, you have the three most dissonant and distant chord extensions. These are the ninth, eleventh, and thirteenth. They typically do note play a role in creating the foundation for a chord, nor do they help to decide whether a chord is minor, Major, or dominant. They also tend to be much less stable than the first, third, fifth, and seventh notes. Although being much less important than the more consonant notes in their function, these notes do, however, help to color chords in interesting ways. A minor 6th and a Major 6th sound incredibly different, all thanks to the slight difference in extension used.

Different Types of Harmony

Plenty has been said about harmony so far in this book, and trust me when I say it's for a good reason. Harmony is both the most important basic building block in music and an incredibly advanced late-stage topic of study. When we discuss harmony, we are talking about the way that notes interact with each other, whether they have dissonant or consonant properties, and what kind of structures that can be shaped and molded into.

Harmony is typically found in four different states:

- Tonal
- Modal
- Polytonal
- Atonal

Below we will quickly run through each type of harmony.

Tonal Harmony

The most common form of harmony that we will run into is known as tonal harmony. Most western music is based around 'tonality' and relies heavily on tonal harmonies. This tonal music is music that is based around a tonic key center, this is a note that takes a central role in a piece of music. Everything eventually ends up gravitating back around to this note. Tonal harmony is our method of understanding the way harmony is harnessed in tonal music. It defines the usage of chords and scales in the context of a key center. Tonal harmony can be split up into three further sub-groups: Chordal, scalar, and chromatic.

Chordal music is primarily based around the usage of chords as its most important harmonic tool. We study and analyze this music by taking note of how chords move around and interact with each other. Chordal music uses chords as its foundation and generally relies on triads to be its backbone.

Scalar music is primarily based around the usage of scales as its most important harmonic tool. This form of harmonic music is understood by studying the way that notes and chords are created from the scales that contain them. Therefore, the most important unit of this music is the scale. This type of music generally uses scales as its base rather than chords of any kind.

Lastly comes Chromatic music. This is primarily based around the twelve note chromatic scale. While very similar to scalar music in many ways, this type of music has a much broader realm due to every scale being found within the larger chromatic scale. In theory, this type of music can enter and leave any other form of harmony as it is based around the most fundamental scale in music.

Modal Harmony

We know that tonal music is always based around some form of note or chord which acts as a key center for a piece of music. This is the case for chordal, scalar, and chromatic music. But while those forms of harmony are always anchored down by a singular central note, modal music is far different. This form of music takes a scale or mode and treats it as a starting point. It then treats all of the notes in that scale or mode as a center to play off of. In other words, this form of music will use an entire scale or mode as its key center.

Polytonality

Polytonal harmony can occupy a space between tonal and modal harmonies. In polytonal harmony it is possible for there to be multiple key centers at any given time. This is possible, in tonal harmony, when more than one note is used as a key center, or when more than one mode or scale is used as a key center in tonal harmony. Regardless of the context, the harmony that results from this is often very dissonant.

Atonal Harmony

In regards to atonal harmonies, there is no recognizable key center. This music was made popular in classical music during the 20th century by Arnold Schoenberg and Anton Webern. This type of music treats all twelve notes like they are key centers. In this type of music, more importance is placed on tones interacting with each other rather than a specific key center. While this music can definitely be difficult to write and listen to, if done correctly it is incredibly beautiful and unique in its sound.

BUILDING UPON YOUR KNOWLEDGE

Chord Progressions - The Basics

Chord progressions are both a simple and complex part of music composition. They fill a basic role in being the most common structure to play chords in, but to be able to use that structure to its fullest extent requires in depth knowledge and experience that beginners will need to develop.

The structure of almost every song is based on chord progressions. This structure is designed to take the listener on a musical journey through the various emotions that a song produces with its tension and resolutions.

As we have already covered, there are three basic families of chords: Tonic, dominant, and subdominant.

The tonic acts as the center of our chord progressions. This is the chord that is often played first and is always representing the key center, the tone that everything else tries to play around and resolve to.

The subdominant acts as the part of a progression that seeks to move the sound away from the tonic center. This can come in the form of quick one chord transitions or longer languid transitions involving multiple chords.

The dominant is the most dissonant part of a progression and acts as the turnaround point where we head back towards the tonic. These chords naturally have the strongest need to move towards the tonic and resolve their dissonant sounds.

When we talk about resolution in chord progressions, we are referring to the act of moving from a non-tonic chord back towards a tonic chord. The initial movement away creates tension which is then removed once the song returns to its tonic center. Without this movement, songs would not have a distinct harmonic direction and would come across as emotionless.

When one chord resolves to the tonic, we call that a cadence. On the occasion that a fifth Major chord resolves to the tonic, we call that a Perfect cadence, which is the basis for one of the most common chord progressions in contemporary music.

When dealing with chord progressions, we use roman numerals to express chords, progressions, and the characteristics of a chord.

Every Major scale key will produce the same sequence of triad chords, and that sequence is as follows:

I (Major) - ii (minor) - iii (minor) - IV (Major) - V (Major) - vi (minor) - vii (diminished)

Try to memorize this sequence as each Major key will produce this sequence and it is important to know it well to play basic chord progressions.

Just like with the Major scale, every minor key will also produce the same sequence of minor triads, this sequence is:

i (minor) - ii (diminished) - III (Major) - iv (minor) - v (minor) - VI (Major) - VII (Major)

You will notice that Majors are capitalized in this system too, minors and diminished are lowercase, and seventh chords have a small 7 next to their numeral.

Common Progressions

In modern music there are quite a few very popular progressions that you may hear very frequently. The most simple and common progression of chords that you may hear is the I - IV - V progression. This sequence of chords uses the I as the tonic, the IV as the subdominant, and the V as the dominant. It also resolves itself by looping back around from V to I, so in many situations it's actually a I - IV - V - I.

For example, in the key of C, this progression would be C - F - G - C.

Another very common progression that you may hear is the ii - V - I progression. Here the ii acts as subdominant, the V acts as the dominant, and the I acts as the tonic.

For example, in the key of C, this progression would be Dm - G - C.

The beautiful thing about chord progressions is that they act as a very useful template to build a song off of. You can pick any key and play any progression, and chances are it will sound very good. Here's a list of some other very popular progressions in modern music:

- I - vi - IV - V
- I - V - IV - V
- I - V - vi - IV
- iii - vi - ii - V
- I - IV - I - V
- I - vi - ii - V
- I - V - ii - V
- I - iii - IV - V
- I - vi - ii - IV

Take note of how in every example, the movement of the progression travels away from a tonic chord, usually through a subdominant, towards a dominant chord. A cadence is then produced when that dominant chord loops around to resolve itself back on the tonic.

How To Extend A Progression

When composing a piece of music, one does not always need to follow a strict progression of chords. There are plenty of occasions when a musician might throw a strange chord or some other trick into a progression to extend it and add something interesting in the process. This usually takes the form of a non-diatonic chord, a key change, a modal adjustment, or some other dissonant trick.

It is also a popular move to extend a progression by adding shorter progressions into the primary progression. Yes, a progression within a progression is a thing.

One example of musicians commonly using these methods is the dominant 7th chord that jazz musicians love to use in their progressions. Often jazz musicians will throw in a dominant 7th chord a fifth above a diatonic chord in their progression.

An example of this in action would be to take the minor ii chord in a progression and replace it with a dominant II7. An example of this would be: I - vi - II7 - V

There are times when chords are played in an ascending or descending sequence on a scale, diatonically or chromatically, so that the musician can move from one part of a chord structure to a different part. A composer can combine adding a 5th to chords and moving diatonically or chromatically, to create a massive amount of creative room for themselves in the chord structure. Keep in mind though, that not every possibility created from this will sound good, this is just a general example of what musicians may do given a certain context.

Musicians will often substitute chords in a progression to change it up or produce a unique sound during certain repetitions of a progression. If a progression is playing again and again in a song, it would make sense to change things up and add a few different chords into it in later progressions otherwise your audience might get bored.

The most common method of doing this would be to simply substitute a tonic, subdominant, or dominant chord in a progression with another chord from the same group.

- Tonic group chords are the first, third, and sixth.
- Subdominant group chords are the second and fourth.
- Dominant group chords are the fifth and seventh.

You will actually see chord substitution used a decent amount in pop music. In fact, The Beatles pioneered its usage in the genre. They would often replace a Major chord with a minor chord in their progressions to provide some more emotion at a later point in the song, before lightening it up again in the next repetition of the progression. This trick actually originated in blues music but has become a mainstay in pop since the 60's.

In blues they would typically use this method by taking a progression which is naturally in a minor key, and add major or dominant chords into the I, IV, and V roles. For example: I - IV - iv - I.

Movement of Tonal Centers

Another common method of extending chord progressions would be through creating temporary harmonic centers. This makes use of the distinction between tonal centers and keys in music. It is completely possible for a song to be based around one key but have many tonal centers. One can play around C Major, then C minor, and then B Major, all while still being in the key of A if that is the key the song is built in overall.

You'll mostly see this technique used by jazz musicians, where a song may be written in a particular key but will travel through multiple tonal centers, sometimes quickly, sometimes through the length of the whole piece. John Coltrane, one of the jazz greats, was famous for having some songs which would travel through as many as nine tonal centers in just a handful of bars before looping back around to normalcy.

Modulation

Key centers and tonal centers take up a separate but related space in the science of chord progressions. When a key changes, we use the term 'modulation' to describe it, we say that the piece has modulated. In cases like this, instead of creating a temporary harmonic center, the whole harmonic structure of a song moves up or down by some number of intervals.

Modulation is a pretty lawless part of chord progressions; there are few rules as to what should and shouldn't be done when modulating a song. Although, one of the basic guidelines to follow is that it usually happens at the start of a repetition in a progression and that whole repetition follows through in that modulated key.

You'll commonly hear modulation, in some form or another, in pop, rock, and country music. This is especially common at the end of a song where one section may be played in a different key to the rest, often a full octave above the original root. This is one of the most basic forms of modulation, playing the same progression only a full octave higher or lower than the rest of the song.

Chord Arpeggios

Chords are created using different notes; you will usually play these notes at the same time, but it is also possible to play them individually but still as a chord, we call this a chord arpeggio.

Arpeggios are a very simple construct, all they are is a chord played in a broken up way. They are very similar to scales; when you learn scales you learn to play a group of notes that fit over a group of chords in a certain key. When you play those scale notes, they'll sound pleasant over those chords. With arpeggios, you learn a group of notes that typically fit over a single chord in a chord progression. This means that you tend to only play arpeggios over that singular chord, and when that chord changes you change your arpeggio too.

Arpeggios are incredibly useful when improvising over chord progressions, they create a premade melody for you to follow. You may be playing a certain scale over a progression, but due to chord substitution, you may run into a chord which does not mesh well with your scale. In this situation, you would simply play the arpeggio of that chord for that section of the song and then switch back to your scale.

A great example of this would be playing a progression such as i - VII - VI - V7. In the key of A minor, these chords would be Am - G - F - E7.

With this progression you would use the A minor scale to solo over the Am, G, and F chords, but when that E7 chord comes along you would have to switch to playing an E7 arpeggio. This means that you'd have to play the E, G#, B, and D chords which are found within that chord.

This is a pretty easy and beginner-friendly way to use arpeggios. You'll eventually want to start thinking of playing arpeggios in a more chordal way, treating each chord in a progression as a separate potential scale to play. By doing this you will stop relying on scales and modes to solo, and you'll start being able to incorporate a lot more chord notes. Doing this will not only make your solos fit and sound more in tune with the chords, but it will also add far more variety and uniqueness to your playing.

If you sit down and analyze some of the most well known solos in history, you will find that they use this exact method. Songs like Sultans of Swing, Hotel California, and Stairway to Heaven all use arpeggios in their guitar solos. These solos are legendary for their incredibly melodic and tonally correct sound, they just feel like they fit perfectly, this is due to the usage of arpeggios.

Arpeggios can also be used to define the outline of the harmony in a song so that you do not have to play chords like you usually would. Often you'll just be able to pick out chord notes and play them in a pattern as the progression moves through the song. This can sound like you are playing the chords, if you play fast enough, even though you are still clearly playing individual notes. It makes for a great melody and sounds very impressive to non-musicians. Arpeggios also allow you to throw in dissonant chords that might otherwise sound terrible if you were to play all of their notes in the same movement.

I think I've said enough to convince you just how useful arpeggios are. Regardless of what instrument you play, they can be a total gamechanger. Take your favorite chords, learn where the notes are, teach yourself how to find them quickly, learn them in some great sounding patterns, and then throw them into your next solo or melody in that key. When it comes to improvising or soloing, remember to focus on the chords you are going to be playing over, learn the context they are being played in and the way that each note sounds over that chord, focussing on certain notes at certain points can have different effects even if they all do sound good.

Chord Progressions - More Advanced Topics

Without chord progressions we would not have tonal harmony as we know it in music. It wasn't until the 50s and 60s that musicians, particularly in jazz, began to use more modal or scalar movements in music. The way music was before then was almost always based around chords of some sort.

Chord progressions tend to be a rather simple topic in music, there are only so many progressions, and for the most part they are easy to understand and use, and you combine, move, change, and divide them according to only a handful of basic rules. The basis of every progression is a simple cycle; you move away from the tonic and then back towards it. This tends to occur through cadences, as we have already mentioned.

The most important cadence in modern music is the V7 - I cadence. In this cadence, a dominant seventh chord is played a fifth above the Major first chord. Although there are a large number of different cadences, they all share the same predominant trait, they act to create tension and then release that tension. This is the general cycle of music, you attempt to create emotion in a piece and then resolve that emotion.

A basic chord progression is built up by a tonic chord, a subdominant which allows for travel away from it, a dominant which is the height of tension, and then a tonic which relieves that tension. Of course, there are many different versions of this, but this is the basic structure that all progressions try to tap into and follow.

Chord Substitutions and Progression Substitutions

When musicians work with chord progressions, and when they improvise over them, they tend to think in terms of chord substitutions. We've talked about this briefly already, but this topic is particularly important to understanding the usage of chord progressions in music. We can extend a progression nearly infinitely by using smart substitutions.

Substituting chords is both one of the easiest and most complicated things to do in music. It's easy to take out one chord and play another in its place, it's difficult to understand and make the most of all the small details that make that act completely effective. In its most simple sense, a chord substitution is reharmonization, and because reharmonizations are part of the basis of melodic variation, chord substitutions are a simple method of creating new ideas in soloing and composition. Chord substitutions can also be very complicated though, they have the potential to be a nightmare for anyone trying to play and improvise on the fly.

We have already talked about how chord substitutions are the process of replacing chords in a progression with one that fills the same role, and one of the easiest ways of doing this is by replacing a chord with another from the same group. But, there are far more ways of substituting chords, a few of which are much more advanced.

For every method of replacing chords, there is potential for more ways of extending compositions, improvising more creatively, and growing your abilities significantly as a player and composer.

Without Changing Root Notes

One simple way to substitute a chord is to change that chord. Sounds simple right? You can keep a chord's bass note and change the other notes to technically replace that chord with another. The most basic way of doing this is what they call quality addition. In this method you simply change a chord through adding a new quality to it, keeping the chord mostly the same except for one note.

For example, you can take a Major seventh chord and add a #11 note to make it into a Maj7#11 chord.

Another easy method is through quality subtraction, the inverse of what was just covered. You can take a minor seventh chord and turn it into a minor triad, a fifth chord, or a minor seventh, just by removing the 5th in it. If you are using extended chords, you can always just remove the extra note to end up with a seventh chord.

These are the two simplest kinds of chord substitution, by rather adding and removing notes in those chords we are technically substituting them, albeit in a lazy way.

As well as adding and subtracting qualities, you can also change them to a different quality, as a method of substituting a chord. You can change a thirteenth chord into a ninth chord by raising the eleven, or you can change a minor ninth into a minor nine flat five by lowering the nine. By lowering or raising notes, you can completely change the outlook of a chord.

Lastly, you can also alter a chord without changing its root note to change its family. You already know that there are three families of chords, and you can identify the family of a chord by looking at the notes inside of it.

- If the chord has a b3 then it is a minor chord.
- If the chord has a Major 3 and a Major 7, then it is a Major chord.
- If the chord has a Major 3 and a Minor 7, then it is dominant.

When you are not sure, just take a look at the scale that includes that chord. If the scale has a Major 3rd and a Minor 7th then it is a dominant chord.

When you change the family of a chord, you change it from minor to Major, from dominant to minor, and whichever other way you choose to move it between families. The chord will stay the same, except for those few notes that make it belong to a certain family.

With Changing Root Notes

You might not want the root note of a chord to always stay the same when substituting. It's pretty common to substitute something to specifically force a new bass movement in a song. In this type of scenario, you need to change the chord completely. The most simple way of doing this is through inversion. By doing this, you will have all of the same notes, just with a different bass note and in a different order.

There is a general rule when working with substituting chords: You always want to try and include two notes of the chord you are removing in the chord that you are replacing it with. As long as you stick to that rule, it's pretty hard to create something that sounds bad.

Similar to inversion, there is a method of substitution called "slash chords". This method takes the body of one chord and merges it with the bass of another. For example, you'll often see it written as Am7/C or some other combination of chords. In this scenario, C is the bass note and Am7 makes up the rest of the notes in the chord.

Combining chords in this way is an important part of polytonality, something we will talk more about later. To keep things simple though, you can substitute a chord by replacing the bass note of one chord with the bass chord of another to create a slash chord. This technique can also be combined with all of those mentioned above to create some complex and interesting substitutions.

Chord Addition

Instead of changing, adding to, or removing from already existing chords in a progression, you can always just add more chords to it. This is a progression substitution rather than a straight chord substitution. In this situation you will choose chords that help to bridge the gap between one chord and another. Although you can always just add chords that have their own role and stand on their own in a progression. These can even go as far as to change the key center of a song for a short period.

For example, you can perform a simple chord addition by taking a iv - V - I in G Major, and adding a ii chord to the beginning of the progression, this means you are adding another subdominant chord. You could also throw in another tonic chord at the beginning, like a vi chord.

Chord Subtraction

The inverse of chord addition is chord subtraction, as I'm sure you can already figure out, this is the process of removing chords from a progression. With this we are also replacing a part of a progression with another, rather than just chord for chord substitution. If you want, you can keep all the chords the same and just remove some chords from certain parts of the progression. Changing the overall feel of a progression without actually changing the chords themselves.

Usually musicians might do this to cut down complex progressions to their most simple form, keeping on the chords most important to the harmony. This can mean only keeping the first tonic chords and the fifth dominant chords. It could also mean keeping only subdominant alongside the third and seventh tonic chords, which makes the song more harmonically mysterious and allows much more room for an improviser to play around in.

Modal Reduction

A technique popularized by the jazz legend Miles Davis, modal reduction is an interesting kind of chord subtraction that has faced a lot of study over the years. This method involves leaving only the chords that are important in defining the modal center of a song. Rather than relying on the root or tonic to be the center of a progression, this type of reduction prefers to prioritize the harmonic center of a scale.

As an example, the chord D Major, E7, B minor, and A Major all have the same modal center. This is not because A Major is the tonic, but rather because they all share notes that can be found in the A Major scale. In this scenario, you can remove all those chords except for the A Major chord and you would still be on the same harmonic center. If you removed them all except for B minor, then the modal center of the song would be the B minor scale.

In modal reduction, you'll commonly see all the chords being removed except for the I and V, this means that all that is left is a structure which a scale is added to. This allows for players to not rely on a chord progression to create movement (which is back and forth between a tonic and dominant), but rather to create movement using scales and modes around a modal center. This means a lot more creative freedom for musicians.

Modal Substitution

By creating a progression as a series of modal centers instead of tonal centers, the possibilities for substituting chords open up massively. Modal substitution allows you to swap one chord for another when they both belong to the same mode or scale.

For example, Cm7 can be used in relation to a modal center like the B Aeolian mode, and that means any chord contained inside of B Aeolian can be used to replace Cm7. The possibilities in regards to reharmonizing are nearly endless with this method of substitution, although it definitely takes a lot of knowledge to harness fully.

Modal Interchange

The last of the modal techniques is modal interchange. This is less to do with the substituting of chords, and more to do with the changing of modal centers. Despite this, the result is still the removing and replacing of chords in a way very similar to chord substitution. What this method entails is rather than using a new chord which shares the same center as the old one, you replace the modal center and create a new chord based on that modal center.

Using this alongside modal substitution opens up the entire harmonic spectrum to a musician, albeit in a way that is rarely used in popular music due to its complexity and dissonance.

THE TOOLS OF THE TRADE

Different Instrument Types

A big part of understanding how music works is also understanding the instruments that it is played on. Without instruments, we wouldn't be able to produce a fraction of the music that we can produce today. While the variety of sounds, frequencies, and different sounds we can produce is nearly infinite, every instrument we use in western music can be classed into one of five major groups: Stringed, brass, woodwind, percussion, and keyboards.

All of these follow the same laws in music and all use the same system of notation. The beauty of music though, is that the way each of these instruments is used and wielded to create sounds, songs, and compositions is wildly different.

Stringed

Stringed instruments are the poster boy of musical instruments. Regardless of whether you're thinking of the mellow double bass of a Jazz troupe, the soaring violins of an orchestra, or the squealing guitar of a rock band, those are some of the most recognizable and culturally significant instruments in history.

Other stringed instruments include: violas, cellos, bass guitars, banjos, bouzoukis, mandolins, and harps.

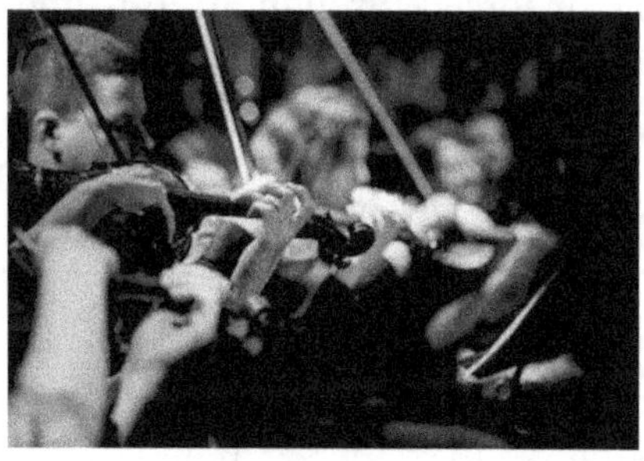

Brass

All brass instruments aren't necessarily brass, in fact any lightweight and easily workable metal can be and is used to create these instruments.

The term brass is just a name used to label a group of metal symphonic wind instruments or any instrument that creates sound by forcing air through the piping of a metal mechanism.

The tone and notes produced by brass instruments are decided by a combination of keys, valves, and slides.

Some examples of brass instruments are: Tubas, trombones, trumpets, baritones, bugles, french horns, and cornets.

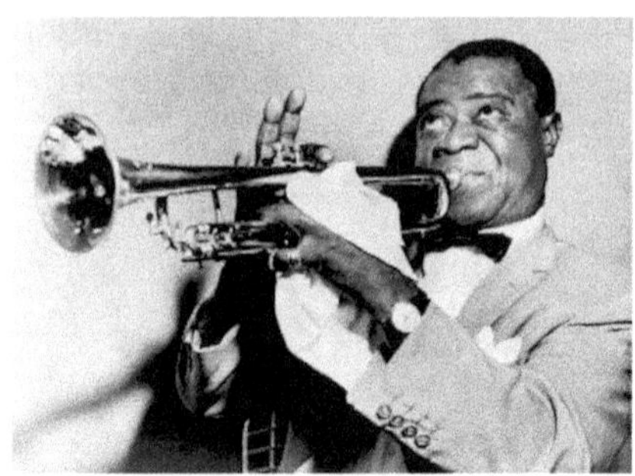

Woodwind

Similar to brass instruments in many ways, woodwinds are often confused with their metallic counterparts. Woodwind instruments are also driven by air forced through an instrument, except instead of a series of valves and mechanisms, these use a series of holes and reeds.

They get their name from the fact that they were originally carved from wood, but nowadays you will find woodwinds made from metal, wood, and molded plastics. Simply put, air goes in one end and depending on which keys or holes you cover, that air escapes through uncovered holes to produce a note.

Some examples of woodwind instruments are: Clarinets, recorders, flutes, oboes, pan flutes, didgeridoos, saxophones, bassoons, and bagpipes.

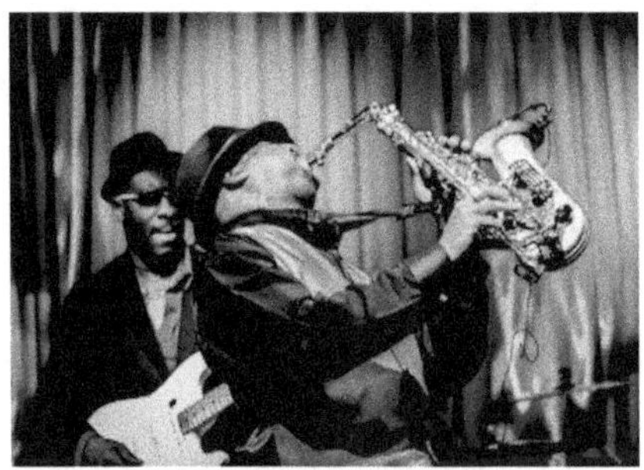

Percussion

Percussion instruments are the outliers when it comes to music theory. They don't create what would typically be considered harmony or melody. Rather than acting as a source of melody, percussion acts as a backing to the sounds of a band or orchestra.

These instruments play a key role in keeping time and rhythm while providing a distinct and progressive driving force behind the more melodic elements of an arrangement. While the most commonly thought of percussion instrument is the drum set, in an orchestral setting there is a wide variety of percussion. Some forms of orchestral percussion can even provide multiple tones and notes depending on the arrangement. Some examples of other percussion instruments are: Bells, anvils, bongos, cymbals, cowbells, gongs, tambourines, and triangles.

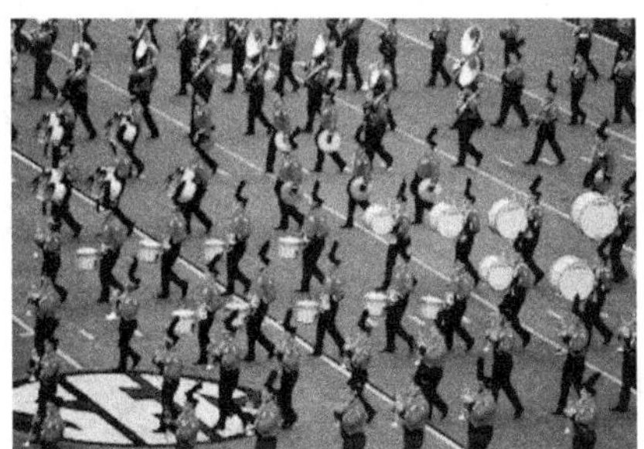

Keyboards

This group of instruments is actually a bit of a grouping of rejects and misfits from many of the other groups. Many of the instruments here have defining features of brass, string, woodwind, and percussion instruments but don't exactly fit into those groups due to the unique way they harness those features.

Take the piano for example, it features the strings of a string instrument, but because the strings are percussed by small hammers, the piano can fall into the percussion group. This same issue holds true with pretty much all of the instruments in this category, the one thing that they do all have in common though, is that they rely on a keyboard to manipulate their sounds.

Some examples of instruments in this group are: Harpsichords, hurdy-gurdys, pipe organs, accordions, synthesizers, and clavichords.

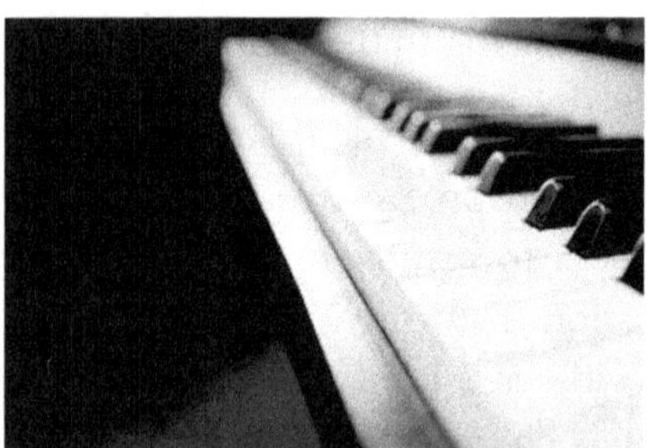

Vocal and Instrument Ranges

Now that we know the different families for each instrument and the way they contribute to music, it is important to know the limits of those instruments. Not every instrument can fill the same role as another, some can only play one note, others are better at harmonies than melodies. Different groups of instruments can even play the same piece of music in different pitches.

One of the main things that sets one instrument apart from another is the range at which it can play in. By knowing the limitations of instruments, you are able to better write music for them. Below we will cover the ranges of most major instruments.

Strings

- Double Bass: C2 - C5
- Cello: C2 - C6
- Viola: C3 - E6
- Violin: G3 - A7
- Bass Guitar: C2 - C5
- Electric Guitar: E2 - E6
- Mandolin: G3 - D7
- Ukulele: C4 - C6

Brass

- Tuba: D1 - F4
- Trombones: A0 - G7
- Horns: F2 - C6
- Trumpets: F3 - C7

Woodwind

- Bassoons: Bb1 - Eb5
- Oboes: A3 - A6
- Clarinets: E3 - C7
- Saxophones: Bb3 - G6
- Flutes: C4 - D7
- Recorders: E1 - G8

Percussion

- Timpani: C2 - D4
- Xylophone: C2 - C7
- Vibraphone: C3 - F6
- Glockenspiel: C5 - F8
- Gong: C2 - G5

Keyboards

- Piano: A0 - C7
- Hammered Dulcimer: D3 - D6
- Organ: C0 - C8
- Harpsichord: F1 - F6

Vocal Ranges

Instruments are great and all, but mankind's oldest and most used instrument is our voices. These come in an infinite variety of different sounds and qualities, with people being capable of creating an incredible range of sounds. These sounds come from our mouths, throats, diaphragms, and all the different techniques used to manipulate the way we push air out of our lungs. Just like other instruments, we also have a way of measuring the range of vocalists.

- Bass: The term bass in music comes from the Latin word "bassus", meaning low. This is the lowest possible vocal range naturally available to humans. These singers produce rich, deep tones and are almost exclusively male.
- Baritone: The word baritone translates roughly to "deep sounding" and lies just above bass in the vocal register. In classical music you will see baritones split into lyric and dramatic baritones, lyric sitting higher in the registry than dramatic. These vocalists are also almost exclusively male.
- Tenor: This is the second highest male vocal range in music. The name comes from the Latin term "tenere" which means to hold, this is due to the fact that tenors are used to hold the melody of a song. The only natural range higher than this is the rare countertenor.
- Alto: This is the lowest of the female vocal ranges, but still much higher than the predominantly male tenor. The term 'alto' is Italian for high.
- Mezzo-soprano: The term mezzo-soprano essentially means "middle-soprano", as the name suggests, they take the middle ground between alto and soprano singers.

- Soprano: This is the highest, brightest, and most angelic sounding range in classical female singing. The term 'soprano' comes from the Latin 'supra' meaning above.
- Falsetto: Lastly comes the falsetto. While many people think this is the highest male singing range, the name explains why it actually isn't. The word 'falsetto' translates to 'false.' This is because singers in this range use a technique to artificially heighten their voices and perform at a register far above their usually natural range.

Different Types of Sheet Music

The primary reason for the existence of music theory is so that musicians had a way of accurately writing down their music for others to repeat. Even without needing to hear the original piece of music, if they can read notation, they can play it in the exact same way that the original composer did.

As long as you know how to read what the original composer wrote, you'll be able to play their song as if you were jamming along with them.

The only issue with notation is, while we do have a somewhat standard form of theory, depending on the genre, instrument, and musicians involved, you may need some vastly different types of sheet music. Below we will summarize some of these forms of sheet music and let you know when you may run into them on your travels.

Lead Sheets

A lead sheet is typically made up of the melody of a song, normally something simple and easy to identify. This type of notation usually also includes the lyrics beneath the written music, along with the names of chords or even chord charts.

This form of sheet music was specifically designed to allow musicians to quickly learn popular music without needing an in-depth knowledge of musical theory. You'll often see books and groupings of lead sheets called "fake books." These allow musicians to quickly pick up an instrument and learn a popular song without having to understand any of the theory behind the composition.

Full Scores

A full score is a type of sheet music that includes notation for every instrument used in that performance. In general, each instrument used in that performance will receive its own staff, this is because instruments usually perform lines of music that differ slightly, and therefore cannot use the same notation.

You'll most commonly see a full score involved in a performance with a large number of musicians and instruments, something like an orchestra or a marching band.

Miniature Scores

A miniature score lives up to its name, this is usually a full score that has been shrunk down from its original size by a large amount. Despite the name though, many miniature scores are as long as a normal musical score, they are often used for breaking down pieces that may be unreasonably long into something of normal length.

Luckily, these scores are almost always only used to be portable or for show. They tend to be less accurate and harder to play off of than full scores, and are therefore not preferred.

Study Scores

A study score is, in essence, a score with doodles on it. These are printed scores that contain extra markings and notes that students may need to fully understand or learn facets of music theory. These are mostly found in textbooks.

Piano Scores

A piano score, as the name suggests, is a score that is specifically meant to be played on a piano. The notation used in this type of sheet music is specifically designed to make life as easy as possible for piano players. This type of sheet is also often used to transpose music that may have meant to be for other instruments into a form of notation that pianists can use.

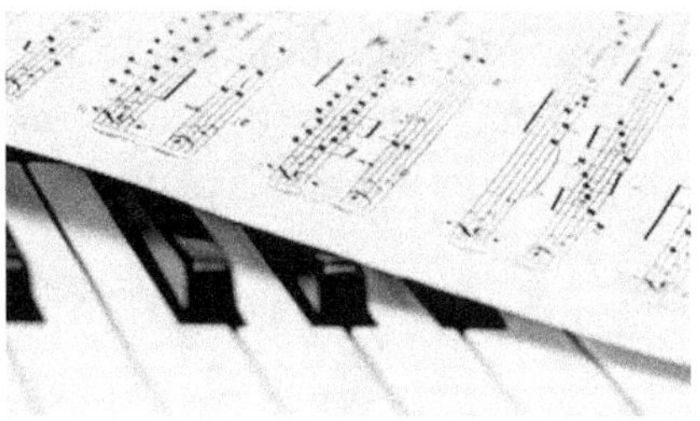

Short Scores

The name given to short scores is actually pretty misleading, these scores are not necessarily short, but rather barren. This is usually the first draft of a full score, a piece of notation containing only the basic harmony and melody of a piece of music. The composer will then take this skeleton of a song and build upon it, adding more instruments, layers, and elements into the mix until they have a full score. These are usually never used in music, in the same way an author will never publish their notepad.

Vocal Scores

As the name suggests, a vocal score is a piece of musical notation typically created for vocalists. It resembles a mixture of a piano score and a lead sheet in many ways, containing the lyrics, the basic melody, and the chord progression of a song. This allows vocalists to keep up with the instrumentation while still focusing on the correct key and lyrics.

Tablature

Tabs, or tablature, is a form of notation that was developed specifically for guitarists and bass guitarists. Rather than using the normal elements of traditional musical theory, tablature uses a number system to denote which note to play on which fret and string. Tabs usually take the form of four to six lines which represent the strings, with numbers to denote which fret the note is in.

The issue with this form of notation is that a composer cannot write specific note values, this means that it's very hard to define the pacing and rhythm of a song in tablature. This can lead to many creative and interesting interpretations of songs. Although this is obviously not ideal, tablature is fantastic due to the fact you need no theoretical education to understand and play along to it.

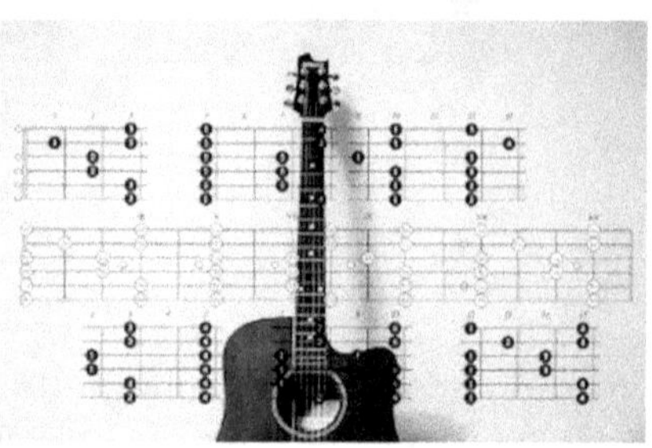

Figured Bass Notation

Lastly, we have figured bass notation. This is a rare type of notation which only features the bass notes of a piece, with numbers providing the intervals needed to accompany that note written below or above the piece. For example, you may see a G note written on the staff with a number four and six below it, that means one must play a fourth and a sixth above that G. This type of notation is almost exclusive to baroque music, so I can't imagine you'll run into it much nowadays.

CONCLUSION

In the world we live in today, it may seem like musical theory has taken a backseat role in the production of music. While it is true that cookie-cutter pop and electronic music has become very prominent in mainstream music, there are still plenty of examples of incredible musical composition floating around. A not particularly new, but still very poignant example of this is John Lennon's *Imagine*. This song has the potential to be a composer's worst nightmare. Within only the first two bars, Lennon goes ahead and throws some of the most fundamental rules of composition out of the window. He uses an I7 that resolves itself a seventh up, rather than down. He leaves a leading note unresolved elsewhere, He plays parallel fifths, and he uses a backward rhythm.

Some of these terms may not be familiar to you, but trust me when I say that most experienced composers would not want those in their songs if they were trying to get people to enjoy their music.

And yet, this is one of the most well known contemporary songs of all time. It has become an anthem for peace and equality across the world and has one of the most recognizable harmonies in all of music. Despite going against many of the most commonly abided by rules in music, this song has become legendary. We have to acknowledge that the rules of music are meant to be broken. In order to create new, innovative, and interesting sounds, we need to be able to push limits and go against what is generally considered normal.

The thing is, without musical theory we wouldn't have any rights and wrongs in music, there wouldn't be any do's or don'ts. This might sound like a good thing right? Isn't art meant to be all about expression? Well yes, but music is equal parts art, science, and psychology. We've made a lot of comparisons between music and science in this book, but psychology?

Let me explain. At the end of the day, the music you hear is defined by the way you interpret it. Some people like hip-hop while others like classical, some like rock while others like jazz. The music you enjoy is decided by your brain, it's decided by some part of your consciousness that seeks to define who you are as a person. The music you listen to, the music you play, and the music you compose are all a part of who you are as a person. Your taste is molded by your experiences and personality, therefore music can be considered a facet of the human psyche.

If you can think of the music you create as a part of who you truly are, you will never find yourself lacking drive or inspiration. Just as you naturally have the drive to eat and sleep, humans naturally want to express themselves, it is a part of you. Through musical theory you can harness that drive, you can direct it to creating something beautiful, something lasting.

THANKS FOR READING

Dear reader,

Thank you for reading *Music Theory for Beginners.*

If you enjoyed this book, please leave a review where you bought it. It helps more than most people think.

Don't forget your FREE book chapters!

You will also be among the first to know of FREE review copies, discount offers, bonus content, and more.

Go to:

https://offers.SFNonfictionBooks.com/Free-Chapters

Thanks again for your support.

REFERENCES

Hollis, B. (2017). *History of Music.* Method-Behind-The-Music.com. https://method-behind-the-music.com/history/history/

Schonbrun, M. (2017). *Music theory 101 - from keys and scales to rhythm and melody, an essential.* Adams Media Corporation.

Stone, S. C. (2019). *Music theory and composition : a practical approach.* Lanham Rowman Et Littlefield.

All images sourced from Pixabay.com

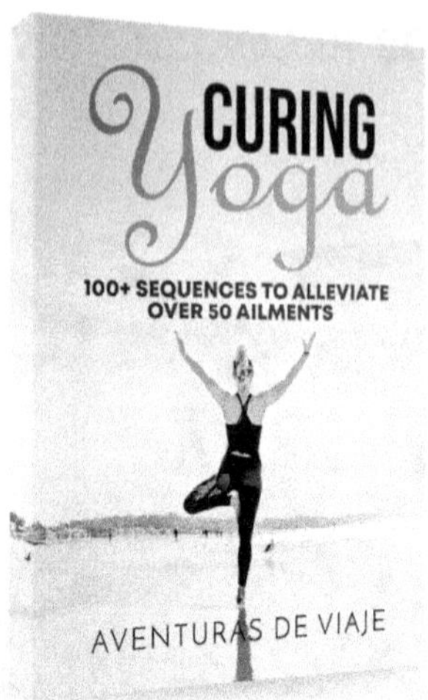

Discover How to Use Yoga as Medicine

Discover how to heal yourself naturally with *Curing Yoga*, because you deserve to feel your best.

Get it now.

www.SFNonfictionBooks.com/Curing-Yoga

ABOUT AVENTURAS

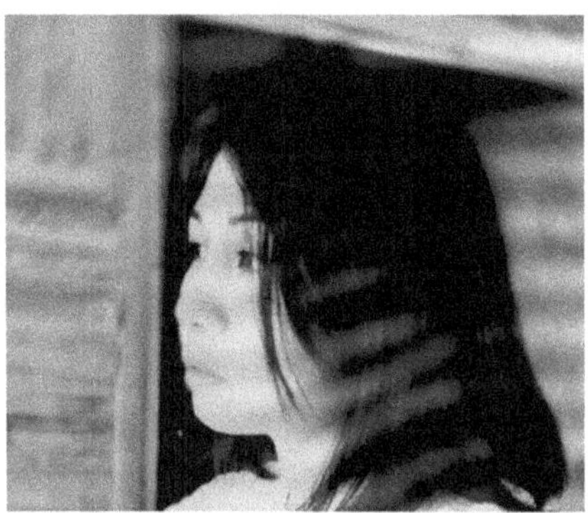

Aventuras has three passions: travel, writing, and self-improvement. She is also blessed (or cursed) with an insatiable thirst for general knowledge.

Combining these things, Miss Viaje spends her time exploring the world and learning. She takes what she discovers and shares it through her books.

www.SFNonfictionBooks.com

amazon.com/author/aventuras

goodreads.com/AventurasDeViaje

facebook.com/AuthorAventuras

instagram.com/AuthorAventuras